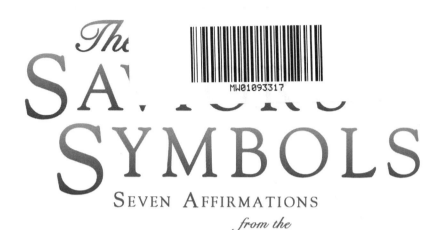

The SAVIOR'S SYMBOLS

SEVEN AFFIRMATIONS
from the
LIFE OF THE MASTER

MARK A. AMACHER

FOREWORD BY ARDETH KAPP

WITH PAINTINGS BY JEFFREY HEIN,
MICHAEL MALM, AND NATHAN PINNOCK

CFI
AN IMPRINT OF CEDAR FORT, INC.
SPRINGVILLE, UTAH

ISBN 13: 978-1-4621-1155-8

Published by CFI, an imprint of Cedar Fort, Inc.
2373 W. 700 S., Springville, UT 84663
Distributed by Cedar Fort, Inc., www.cedarfort.com

LIBRARY OF CONGRESS CATALOGING-IN-PUBLICATION DATA

Amacher, Mark A., 1955- author.
The Savior's symbols : seven affirmations from the life of the Master / Mark A. Amacher.
    pages cm
Includes bibliographical references and index.
Summary: Explores how and where the Savior used the symbols he selected to teach and testify of his life and mission.
ISBN 978-1-4621-1155-8 (alk. paper)
1. Jesus Christ--Teachings. 2. Jesus Christ--Words. 3. Symbolism in the Bible. 4. Church of Jesus Christ of Latter-day Saints--Doctrines. 5. Mormon Church--Doctrines. I. Title.

BX8643.J4A43 2013
232.9'5--dc23
                              2012044972

Cover design by Rebecca J. Greenwood
Cover design © 2013 Lyle Mortimer
Edited and typeset by Emily S. Chambers

Printed in the United States of America

10 9 8 7 6 5 4 3 2 1

Printed on acid-free paper

For Patti and all Saints

All royalties from this publication are donated to
The Church of Jesus Christ of Latter-day Saints
or
The Perpetual Missionary Foundation for
The Church of Jesus Christ of Latter-day Saints
www.PerpetualMissionaryFoundation.org

Contents

Foreword

SYMBOLISM IS USED TO ENRICH A PERSON'S LEARNING according to the spiritual preparation of the one ready to receive.

Orson F. Whitney explained, "The Universe is built on symbols, lifting our thoughts from man to God, from earth to heaven, from time to eternity . . . God teaches with symbols; it is His favorite way of teaching" (*Improvement Era*, August 1927, 851).

The style of writing in this book invites thoughtful contemplation that is personal and purposeful, appropriate to the message. Many events are beautifully portrayed with visual imagery such as the wine at the wedding feast, the color red in the Savior's apparel when He returns in glory, and the preparation of sacrificial lambs on Passover eve. As members of The Church of Jesus Christ of Latter-day Saints, we are familiar with sacred symbols like the sacrament we partake of each week as a reminder of our covenants with the Lord and His promised blessings.

Reading this book can increase your desire to know Him and to become like Him through a deeper understanding of His life and ministry. It invites a rich experience in drawing closer to our Savior—the Master Teacher—through His symbols.

—Ardeth Kapp

Preface

"And now, behold, I say unto you: This is the plan of salvation
unto all men, through the blood of mine Only Begotten, who
shall come in the meridian of time."

—Moses 6:62

THIS BOOK EXAMINES THE SAVIOR'S SELECTION AND USE OF
symbols in his personal teachings and mortal ministry. He
has blessed us with many names and representative symbols,
only a few of which we will be able to explore in this work.

All creation bears record of the Savior and His mission.
This applies to names, symbols, and titles, as well as all physical things. Sometimes we need to look deeply to find the correct connections and representation; other times they are more
simple and straightforward, as with the symbols the Lord
selected in His teaching and testimony. It is not insignificant
that the premortal Jehovah taught Adam, "All things have their
likeness, and all things are created and made to bear record
of me, both things which are temporal, and things which are
spiritual; things which are in the heavens above, and things
which are on the earth, and things which are in the earth, and
things which are under the earth, both above and beneath: all
things bear record of me" (Moses 6:63).

All His symbols and names orient and direct us to Him.

His life is exemplary and illuminating; His message is captivating, inspiring, and motivating; but His mission—His mission is singular and central, individual and infinite. His eternal Atonement is the focal point of all creation and mediates our journey from premortal beginning to post resurrection end (see chapter 7). It is to this end that all His symbols direct us, illuminating the path that returns through Christ to our Father in Heaven.

As we begin our study of the Savior's symbolism, we are aided if we begin with the end of his mortal mission in mind. His life culminated in the central act of time, the focal point of universal history. Without Christ's infinite Atonement, innumerable worlds of his creation and the inhabitants thereof would be lost forever, having no hope of redemption from their mortal, fallen state. As prophesied in the book of Moses, Christ came in the meridian of time to this particular earth, "in the days of wickedness and vengeance," to be humbly born and to viciously die (Moses 7:60).

Infinite physical and spiritual worlds (Alma 26:37; D&C 138:18–19) witnessed the signs of his birth and waited in faith, anticipating his mortal ministry and ultimate sacrifice. As He grew in wisdom and stature, He manifested a physical and spiritual depth we can only hope to fully comprehend or appreciate in this life. Because He was living a pure and perfect life, He possessed a fulness of faith pertaining to His life's mission and message. As He descended to the waters of the river Jordan, Jesus knew that His public ministry was about to commence. His ministry, like His life, would be perfect. He would teach with divine authority, richly presenting his message and personal witness. He would use symbolic imagery, parables, and foreshadowing to help the least of us come to understand his divine mission as Christ, the Atoning One (see chapter 5).

Jesus was baptized "in Bethabara beyond Jordan where John was baptizing" (John 1:28). In addition to fulfilling all righteousness (Matthew 3:15), the Lord was foreshadowing His mortal life's mission. Submitting Himself in all things to the will of His Father, He descended to the lowest physical location on the planet to be baptized. This physical descent and symbolic burial in the depths of the water represented his earthly condescension and approaching Atoning death. He would suffer the pains of all as He "descended below all things, in that He comprehended all things, that He might be in all and through all things, the light of truth" (D&C 88:6). Over the next forty-two months, He would call His disciples, teach His gospel, heal the sick, and restore truth; establishing His church and conferring authority including priesthood keys. He would lift, encourage, correct, chasten, and condemn; all while testifying of Himself as directed by His Father in Heaven. He would give all He had and in the end, He would suffer all things, so that we may receive all things.

As He approached His final week in mortality,

> Nothing remained for Him on earth but the torture of physical pain and the poignancy of mental anguish. All that the human frame can tolerate of suffering was to be heaped upon [Him] . . . every misery that cruel and crushing insult can inflict was to weigh heavy on His soul. . . . Pain in its

acutest sting, shame in its most overwhelming brutality, all the burden of the sin and mystery of man's existence in its apostasy and fall; this was what He must now face in all its most inexplicable accumulation.[1]

His perfect Atonement wasn't just a casual action of an all-powerful God, enduring a physical discomfort during a short temporal interlude. Jesus inherited from His mortal mother all the capacity of human suffering, grief, and pain combined with the character, abilities, and divine nature of His Heavenly Father. He had a unique capacity not only to suffer and endure but to overcome infinite and eternal punishments. "How sore you know not, how exquisite you know not, yea, how hard to bear you know not. . . . Nevertheless, glory be to the Father, and I partook and finished my preparations unto the children of men" (D&C 19:15–19).

Perhaps most sobering is the realization that He did it all voluntarily (Luke 22:42). With just one word, one divine declaration, He could have ended it. "He was oppressed and he was afflicted. . . yet he opened not his mouth" (Isa. 53:7). Finally, His perfect purifying Atonement wasn't just His infinite suffering through Gethsemane and a Roman crucifixion, He had lived every telestial day perfectly in a world so wicked, so perverse, it would crucify its very creator (Eph. 3:9). His lesser law, like the water that He turned to wine, was replaced with something greater—"Full-fillment" or exaltation centered on Christ through the enabling grace of His Atonement (see chapter 1).

Knowing all this from the beginning, we find in His

teachings and symbolism repeated references to his mission as Savior and Redeemer. As we examine different events in the Lord's ministry, we observe Him skillfully referring to familiar symbols that illuminated and foreshadowed His Atonement. They draw us to Him, filling us with light and love, with gratitude and humility.

In each chapter, we consider symbols the Savior selected to teach us of Him. He did not choose a fish, a bleeding heart, or even the familiar cross to represent Him; rather, He chose familiar common symbols that inspire and instruct, symbols that open a pondering mind to rich insights and layered understandings.

Scriptures, hymns, sacred art, and personal photos, which relate to the symbolism and doctrines discussed, are included. They are intended to reference and reverence His symbols and sacrifice.

This work invites you to think expansively and to feel differently about Christ. His symbols inspire feelings and insights as you study his words. While you ponder the circumstances and messages of each symbol, you will, if you choose, come to know Him better. At some point during your reading, you will have a renewed witness of and a deep feeling of gratitude for the Savior. Pay attention to communication from the Holy Ghost, listening for specific impressions regarding how you should act. You may feel Him working with you, working in you, and blessing others through you. As you act on your impressions, you will come to testify how He individually cares for each person, every family, and all of humanity. Jesus loves you with unimaginable compassion. His actions perfectly express His love. His chosen symbols are lampposts and guide signs that illuminate His straight, narrow path, leading to the tree of life and the precious fruit thereof (see chapter 5).

As we personalize His sacrifice, we may come to know His will for each of us. When our desires focus on Christ, our capacity for good multiplies as the Holy Ghost directs and sanctifies us. If we seek and receive His gifts of the Spirit, we act with greater capacity, utilizing our innate abilities and character to bless the lives of others. As we serve, we are drawn ever closer to our Lord; gathering and restoring Israel to His temples and covenants, binding us to Him and to each other; enabling us to become at one with Him and one with Heavenly Father's celestial family.

How infinite that wisdom,
The plan of Holiness,
That made salvation perfect,
And veiled the Lord in flesh,
To walk upon his footstool,
And be like man, almost,
In his exalted station,
And die, or all was lost.

"O God, The Eternal Father," Hymns, no. 175
verse 4.

CHAPTER 1
Wine

"I AM the true vine, and my Father is the husbandman. . .
Abide in me, and I in you. As the branch cannot bear fruit
of itself, except it abide in the vine; no more can ye, except ye
abide in me."

—John 15:1, 4

IT WAS THE LAST WEEK OF THE SAVIOR'S MORTAL MINISTRY, the week of Jewish Passover. Jesus had gathered His disciples together in an upper room for His final instruction and blessing as the mortal Messiah. They had experienced much together; however, what was coming next, He must endure alone.

Jesus knew "that his hour was come that he should depart out of this world unto the Father" (John 13:1). These loyal men would bear the burden of the Church and kingdom on earth after He ascended to His Father. They would preach His gospel to the gentiles and bear apostolic testimonies of Jesus Christ, the Son of God. He would miss them. He loved them as only He could. Now His time was short, and He must teach them a few last lessons on service and sacrifice, completing His mortal instruction to them. He was preparing them, even as He prepared Himself, for what was soon to come.

As they were eating, Jesus took bread and wine as testaments of His pending sacrifice and blessed and passed them to His chosen friends. "And he took the cup, and gave thanks, and gave it to them, saying, Drink ye all of it; for this is my blood of the new testament, which is shed for many for the remission of sins" (Matt. 26:27–28).

No matter how these events may have been interpreted or represented to you in the past, a clear understanding of what the symbolism evokes contrasts significantly with Hollywood's common portrayal of Jesus as a type of detached, mystical savant. John's Gospel evidences an engaging, dynamic, even social personality who was keenly aware and personally interested in everyone around Him.

As with all teaching, His greatest lessons were taught by example. His many miracles—such as physical healings and restorations from death—were all administered to individuals. This style of personal ministering illustrates the great work of redemption in all dispensations where faith, repentance, baptism, and other saving ordinances of salvation are received as individuals. Thus, as He administered the first sacrament to each of His disciples, He explained, "I say unto you, I will not drink henceforth of this fruit of the vine, until that day when I drink it new with you in my Father's kingdom" (Matt. 26:29). After so much time together, this was a sobering declaration.

The wine He blessed and passed was a common commodity used for drink and for medicinal purposes. It was also deeply symbolic. It represented fertility, prosperity, abundance, celebration, and blessings. As we shall see, Jesus had previously used wine as a symbol of the qualitative results of His works while also using the wine production process as representative and illuminative of His Atonement. To use wine as a symbolic emblem of His blood and to say that He would never partake of wine again in this life was to make a powerful statement about Himself and about His Apostles' changing relationship with Him. Things were never to be "as they were" before this last supper together.

Early in His mortal ministry, Jesus had attended a marriage in Cana where He had turned water into wine. Interestingly, many biblical scholars identify this occurrence as the first recorded miracle of Christ's mortal ministry. By way of contrast, when the Prophet Joseph Smith was once asked, "What was the first miracle the Lord performed?" he answered insightfully, "The creation!"

We know that the organization of this earth and the other worlds the Lord brings into existence are acts of creation. A marriage is also an act of creation. As "The Family: A Proclamation to the World" states, "Marriage is ordained of God,"[2] and as such, it is sanctioned by the Lord as an act of creation. Still today, many Jewish families refer to a wedding event by saying that they "made a wedding," a clear reference to the understanding belief in a creative act.

A wedding in Israel was always a big social event, especially in a small village like Cana of Galilee. Family and close friends had probably come from the neighboring villages of Magdala, Nazareth, Capernaum, Gennesaret, or Tabgha. Jewish weddings were usually held on a Tuesday, "on the third day of the week" (JST, John 2:1). This tradition was observed because the Lord had pronounced a "double blessing" on the third day of creation by stating that it was "good" twice (Gen. 1:9–13). As a result, it was widely believed that a marriage union would be doubly blessed if it were performed on the third day of the week, a tradition still observed today in more orthodox Jewish communities.

Weddings were major celebrations lasting from several days to as long as two weeks. In rural Galilee, a wedding could easily unite the limited number of local families into extended relationships of rich association and family friendships. Each marriage event, as well as the major feasts and observances of the year, were celebrated together as part of a family's history and tradition. This wedding at Cana was such an occasion. It was cause for much joy and celebration. From the scriptural text recorded in the Gospel of John, we recognize that the family of Jesus had a close and personal interest in this wedding. Mary, the mother of Jesus, was responsible in some way for the comfort and hospitality of the guests. When the supply of local wine ran out, the servers looked to Mary for direction. Since Jesus and His brethren were there, it was to become a memorable occasion—not just because of the wedding celebration, but also for the rich lessons, precious insights, and gospel symbolism taught by the Savor early in His ministry.

Jesus had recently been baptized. He had then called and organized His disciples. He had also begun teaching them and preparing them for future leadership, but as yet He had not performed any public miracles. The record indicates that the time had not yet come to begin His public demonstrations or declarations. In this circumstance, we see Him joining the wedding celebration and interacting with family and friends. He was social, engaging, supportive, and willing to assist. It was in this attitude that "Jesus said unto her [His mother], Woman, what wilt thou have me to do for thee? that will I do; for mine hour is not yet come. His mother said unto the servants, Whatsoever he saith unto you, see that ye do it" (JST, John 2:4–5).

The law of Moses prescribed detailed observances regarding diet and cleanliness. Some were practical while others were ceremonial; all were symbolic. To observe and keep the law, the Jews would wash as prescribed by the requirements of the law. At this house in Cana, there stood six stone water pots, reservoirs of water for the purpose of ceremonial washings "after the manner of the purifying of the Jews, containing two or three firkins apiece" (John 2:6). A firkin was approximately 9.5 US gallons, so these six pots yielded a conservative total volume of 135–150 gallons! The large quantity of water symbolized the commitment and desire of the household, the tradition if you will, to be clean and to observe the law. It might also have been seen as a polite gesture to provide a convenient place to perform the rituals of ceremonial washing (as it is today in modern Israel).

The Lord chose this moment and this circumstance to manifest His first recorded public miracle while teaching symbolic lessons. What were His lessons and what effect did it have on His new disciples? The symbolism of wine and the teaching circumstances provide insight to His message, testimony, and mission.

The premortal Messiah had commanded that the laws He gave to Moses be observed. Jesus, the Messiah, was the lawgiver! He had provided the lesser law, the law of cardinal commandments, as a schoolmaster to instruct and to point Israel to Himself as the mortal Messiah who would come in the meridian of time. Now was that time. He had come to fulfill His own law. The miracle of the marriage wine would symbolize His fulfillment of the law while foreshadowing and symbolically presenting how it would be accomplished.

"Jesus saith unto them, Fill the waterpots with water. And they filled them up to the brim" (John 2:7). Jesus first physically and metaphorically filled the pots with cleansing and purifying water, thus ensuring that the lesser law was observed. The full water pots also suggest a "fulness" of blessings that results from obeying the law of the Lord. He then transformed the full containers of water to wine, one of the future emblems of the sacrament. The symbolism clearly referenced His Atonement as the manner in which He would fulfill the law, satisfy the demands of justice, extend divine mercy, and bless all His creations. Not only was new wine produced by or through Him, but the water was also done away, fulfilled in Him. The law of Moses, the law of sacrifice, was replaced with the higher law of Christ through His last great, infinite, and eternal sacrifice. The water was "added upon" just as the law of Moses was added upon through Christ's law. It became more complete, full, and complex—a more fruitful liquid. It now had greater ability to satisfy; it was more enjoyable, more bountiful, and much more abundant. It was worthy to be presented at this wedding banquet even as He will be worthily presented at a final marriage banquet—the marriage supper of the Bridegroom where wine may be served in infinite abundance.

The miracle of the marriage wine clearly symbolized Christ's Atonement and represents His blood sacrifice (Heb. 9:14–15). But there are also other more subtle messages layered in the wine's characteristics and attributes. They speak to us about the quality and quantity of His work: "And he saith unto them, Draw out now, and bear unto the governor of the feast. And they bare it. When the ruler of the feast had tasted the water that was made wine, . . . [he] called the bridegroom, and saith unto him, Every man at the beginning doth set forth good wine; and when men have well drunk, then that which is worse: but thou hast kept the good wine until now" (John 2:8–10).

The reaction by the governor of the marriage suggests that the wine Jesus provided was the best wine, of the finest quality, and it was provided in abundance. The quantity of wine provided—upwards of 150 gallons for a group who had already been drinking freely—would have been more than sufficient to satisfy the needs of this small gathering. The Lord's Atonement required the best and most precious blood of all ages, the best offering possible, both in quality and in quantity. "God will provide himself a lamb" (Gen. 22:8; see chapter 6).

For it is expedient that an atonement should be made . . . a great and last sacrifice; yea, not a sacrifice of man, neither of beast, neither of any manner of fowl; for it shall not be a human sacrifice; but it must be an infinite and eternal sacrifice. . . . And behold, this is the whole meaning of the law [of Moses], every whit pointing to that great and last sacrifice; and that great and last sacrifice will be the Son of God, yea, infinite and eternal. (Alma 34: 9–10, 14)

So another testimony provided by the wine miracle is that the Atonement, in its quality and quantity, is more than sufficient to satisfy the demands of justice and to balance the personal accounts of all who come unto Christ. The Lord Himself declared, "I am come that they might have life, and that they might have *it* more abundantly" (John 10:10; emphasis added). This miracle was a powerful first demonstration of His power to provide abundant blessings through His life and Atonement.

The context of the wine miracle also offers instructive symbolism through its association with the wedding feast. The Lord used the imagery of a wedding feast, and especially of the Bridegroom at the last day, as an occasion to symbolically gather the faithful in to supper with Him. All who are sufficiently prepared to meet Him—those who have accepted Him and have fully repented of their sins; those who have their lamps filled with oil, their wicks trimmed, and extra oil available (see chapter 5); those who are prepared in all things— they will be admitted into the presence of the Lord. There they will sit down with Abraham, Isaac, Jacob, and Joseph. There, He who has overcome all things will provide bread and wine in abundance (see chapter 3). This last great banquet will be real, the promises sure, and the Host—the Holy One of Israel.

The scripture record affirms that the Lord accomplished significant objectives in this "first" miracle. For example, He was able to tenderly assist and help His mother while instructing and building faith in His disciples: "This beginning of miracles did Jesus in Cana of Galilee, and manifested forth his glory; and the faith of his disciples was strengthened in him" (JST, John 2:11).

Grapes grow in great abundance in the Holy Land. The soil is fertile and the climate perfect for grape vineyards at moderate altitudes. The ancient process for wine production commenced at harvest time. The grapes were gathered and brought to a winepress. The "press" was made of stone and had a lower and an upper basins or vat into which the grapes were placed. A group of men, an ox, or some other beast of burden was employed to tread on or "step out" the grapes in the upper vat. This was called "pressing." Linen cloth was wrapped around the person's or animal's legs to protect them from the sticks and vines that could cut, scrape, and tear the flesh while laboring.

The process was exhausting and could take many hours to complete. All the contents in the wine vat must be worked by pressing to reclaim the wine. The grape juice pressed out from the upper vat was drawn out and collected in the lower chamber, leaving the upper vat with a mash of matted vine, twigs, crushed grape skins, and seeds. The flow of wine started out quite rapidly at first but slowed to a trickle as the last of the grapes were squeezed out. The labor was not complete until the flow stopped and all the wine that would be claimed had been drawn.

When the pressing was complete, the linen cloth employed to protect the flesh was stained a vibrant red wine color. The stain was a symbol of the harvest and a token of the effort required to produce wine. The pressing labor was so exhausting and taxing that several men usually assisted each other by taking turns so that each worker had a chance to rest and recover somewhat from the effort. Even animals were rested and rotated in this way; otherwise, it was difficult to maintain balance in the wine vat and not fall from the physical effort to press out wine in this ancient way.

Try to imagine an old stone winepress in ancient Israel. How would it feel to press out grapes without any assistance? How difficult to tread the winepress alone? It might be easy at first, but as time progresses, your fatigue and heaviness increases as the flow of wine decreases. More pressure is needed to complete the job, more effort required. Minutes stretch into hours. With exhausting fatigue, sweat, and toil your strength is drawn out as the remains of the pressing vat tear at your heavy, aching, burning legs. Your breathing is heavy; your lungs burn. The winepress is uneven, and it is difficult for you to maintain your balance. You stagger, stumble, and fall frequently in your fatigue. You appear to be drunk as you "reel to and fro" in the winepress. After hours of toil, if you complete the task, you are scratched, cut, bruised, and soaked through with sweat. With matted hair and red-stained garments, completely exhausted, you are hardly able to move or speak. The Lord's wine, symbolic of His atoning blood, was pressed out alone, under intense pressure, drop-by-drop, step-by-step, balancing eternal justice with atoning mercy.

This is powerful imagery. The Savior's revelation to the Prophet Joseph Smith of His glorious Second Coming includes references to winepress symbolism:

> Who is this that cometh down from God in heaven with dyed garments; yea, from the regions which are not known, clothed in his glorious apparel, traveling in the greatness of his strength? . . . And the Lord shall be red in his apparel, and his garments like him that treadeth in the wine-vat. . . And his voice shall be heard: I have trodden the winepress alone, and have brought judgment upon all people; and none were with me. (D&C 133:46, 48, 50; see also Isa. 63:1–3)

Wine is also a fitting symbol of Christ because of its great worth. It is valued because it is not easily produced. Thus, the effort required to achieve wine's unique characteristics makes it a fitting emblem for the sacrament. The words *sacrament* and *sacrifice* have the same Latin root—*sacer,* meaning "holy" or "to make sacred." They both point to the Savior and His Atonement as the means to make us sacred.

Since the time of Adam, the Lord commanded His people to offer sacrifices in similitude of Him. It pointed forward, looking ahead to His central act. Sacrifices were performed in a prescribed manner, teaching us of the Atonement and of the Atoning One (see chapter 6). Sacrifices required the first-lings of the flock, without blemish and without spot, with no broken bones, with their blood shed and the life-giving blood sprinkled on the north side of the altar. All these and many other observances of the law of Moses (like the Passover itself) pointed to Christ as the last great and terrible sacrifice.

> Now as Jesus and his apostles celebrated the Feast of the Passover, which itself was part of the ancient sacrificial system, a new ordinance was in the making. The paschal lambs were testifying for the last time that the Lamb of God should be sacrificed for the sins of the world. The hour had come for the great and last sacrifice, and once the Son of God had been lifted upon the altar of the cross there would be no further need for an ordinance looking forward to that day. . . . As sacrifice was thus to cease with the occurrence of the great event toward which it pointed, there must needs be a new ordinance to replace it, an ordinance which also would center the attention of the saints on the infinite and eternal atonement. And so Jesus, celebrating [observing] the feast of the Passover, thus dignifying and fulfilling the law to the full, initiated the sacrament of the Lord's Supper. Sacrifice stopped and sacrament started. It was the end of the old era and the beginning of the new.[3]

This was the meridian of time. It was His time. This was the central act of all history—Christ's prime meridian, His pinnacle of love. His new sacrament included bread and wine, symbols of His abundance, freely and abundantly given. These symbols were offered willingly, blessing all who seek and receive Him. Through Him, they make us sacred as He is sacred. His atoning blood and acts of grace can make us holy, as He is holy. "And he said unto them, This [wine] is in remembrance of my blood which is shed for many, and the new testament which I give unto you; for of me, ye shall bear record unto all the world. And as oft as ye do this ordinance, ye will remember me in this hour that I was with you, and drank with you of this cup, even the last time in my ministry" (JST, Mark 14:23–24).

At this last supper with His chosen Apostles, in an obscure chamber in the upper city of Jerusalem, Jesus had washed their feet and prayed to the Father for them. He had implemented the sacrament and taught them all that His Father had commanded Him. It was now time.

"And when they had sung an hymn, they went out into the mount of Olives" (Matt. 26:30).

We'll sing all hail to Jesus' name,
And praise and honor give,
To him who bled on Calvary's hill,
And died that we might live.

The bread and water represent,
His sacrifice for sin;
Ye saints, Partake and testify,
Ye do remember Him.

"We'll Sing All Hail to Jesus' Name," Hymns,
no. 182, verses 1, 4.

Commentary

ABINADI'S MESSAGE AND THE LAW OF MOSES

The law of Moses was fulfilled in the mission of Jesus Christ and His infinite Atonement. We have seen how wine can symbolize that sacred sacrifice. One of the greatest testimonies of the law of Moses and the central role of the Savior was taught by the Nephite prophet Abinadi. He was brought before the wicked King Noah and his priests to be questioned and accused for prophesying and preaching repentance as he had been commanded by the Lord. The priests "began to question him [Abinadi], that they might cross him, that thereby they might have wherewith to accuse him; but he answered them boldly, and withstood all their questions, yea, to their astonishment; for he did withstand them in all their questions, and did confound them in all their words" (Mosiah 12:19).

Abinadi asked the priests what they taught. They replied, "We teach the law of Moses" (Mosiah 12:28). Abinadi then challenged them, saying, "What know ye concerning the law of Moses? Doth salvation come by the law of Moses? What say ye? And they answered and said that salvation did come by the law of Moses." (Mosiah 12:31–32) When Abinadi rebuked them for not teaching obedience to the law, they sought to take his life.

> And now when the king had heard these words, he said unto his priests: Away with this fellow, and slay him; for what have we to do with him, for he is mad. And they stood forth and

attempted to lay their hands on him; but [Abinadi] withstood them, and said unto them: Touch me not, for God shall smite you if ye lay your hands upon me, for *I have not delivered the message* which the Lord sent me to deliver; neither have I told you that which ye requested that I should tell; therefore, God will not suffer that I shall be destroyed at this time. (Mosiah 13:1–3; emphasis added)

Abinadi could not be touched until he had delivered his message, given his testimony, and warned the people of the consequences of their disobedience.

What was Abinadi's message? He declared,

Ye see that ye have not power to slay me, therefore I finish my message. . . . And now ye have said that salvation cometh by the law of Moses. I say unto you that it is expedient that ye should keep the law of Moses as yet; but I say unto you, that the time shall come when it shall no more be expedient to keep the law of Moses. And moreover, I say unto you, that *salvation doth not come by the law alone; and were it not for the atonement, which God himself shall make for the sins and iniquities of his people, that they must unavoidably perish, notwithstanding the law of Moses*. . . . But behold, I say unto you, that all these things were types of things to come. . . . And now, did they understand the law? I say unto you, Nay, they did not all understand the law; and this because of the hardness of their hearts; for they understood not that there could not any man be saved except it were through the redemption of God. *For behold, did not Moses prophesy unto them concerning the coming of the Messiah, and that God should redeem his people?* Yea, and even all the prophets who have prophesied ever since the world began—have they not spoken more or less concerning these things? Have they not said that God himself should come down among the children of men, and take upon him the form of man, and go forth in mighty power upon the face of the earth? Yea, and have they not said also that he should bring to pass the resurrection of the dead, and that he, himself, should be oppressed and afflicted?

And now Abinadi said unto them: *I would that ye should understand that God himself shall come down among the children of men, and shall redeem his people.* And because he dwelleth in flesh he shall be called the Son of God, and having subjected the flesh to the will of the Father, being the Father and the Son—The Father, because he was conceived by the power of God; and the Son, because of the flesh; thus becoming the Father and Son—And they are one God, yea, the very Eternal Father of heaven and of earth. And thus the flesh becoming subject to the Spirit, or the Son to the Father, being one God, suffereth temptation, and yieldeth not to the temptation, but suffereth himself to be mocked, and scourged, and cast out, and disowned by his people.

And after all this, after working many mighty miracles among the children of men, he shall be led, yea, even as Isaiah said, as a sheep before the shearer is dumb, so he opened not his mouth. Yea, even so he shall be led, crucified, and slain, the flesh becoming subject even unto death, the will of the Son being swallowed up in the will of the Father. And thus God breaketh the bands of death, having gained the victory over death; giving the Son power to make intercession for the children of men—Having ascended into heaven, having the bowels of mercy; being filled with compassion toward the children of men; standing betwixt them and justice; having broken the bands of death, taken upon himself their iniquity and their transgressions, having redeemed them, and satisfied the demands of justice. . .

And now, ought ye not to tremble and repent of your sins, and *remember that only in and through Christ ye can be saved? Therefore, if ye teach the law of Moses, also teach that it is a shadow of those things which are to come—Teach them that redemption cometh through Christ the Lord, who is the very Eternal Father.* Amen. (Mosiah 13:7, 27–28, 32–35; 15:1–9; 16:13–15; emphasis added)

The lesser law, like the water that was turned to wine, was replaced with something greater—"Full-fillment" or exaltation centered on Christ through the enabling grace of the Atonement. Abinadi taught this truth regarding Christ and the law of Moses and sealed his testimony with his death by fire. His testimony is still in effect to all who hear his testimony. His is one of many voices from the dust that declare redemption through Christ.

THE SAVIOR PROCLAIMS THAT THE LAW IS FULFILLED

Clearly and directly the Lord proclaimed at Bountiful the fulfillment of the law of Moses and its intent—to align us with Christ. Nephi wrote,

And it came to pass that when Jesus had said these words he perceived that there were some among them who marveled, and wondered what he would concerning the law of Moses; for they understood not the saying that old things had passed away, and that all things had become new. And he said unto them: Marvel not that I said unto you that old things had passed away, and that all things had become new. Behold, I say unto you that the law is fulfilled that was given unto Moses. *Behold, I am he that gave the law, and I am he who covenanted with my people Israel; therefore, the law in me is fulfilled, for I have come to fulfil the law; therefore it hath an end. Behold, I do not destroy the prophets, for as many as have not been fulfilled in me, verily I say unto you, shall all be fulfilled.* And because I said unto you that old things have passed away, I do not destroy that which hath been spoken concerning things which are to come. For behold, the covenant which I have made with my people is not all fulfilled; but the law which was given unto Moses hath an end in me. *Behold, I am the law, and the light. Look unto me, and endure to the end, and ye shall live; for unto him that endureth to the end will I give eternal life.* Behold, I have given unto you the commandments; therefore keep my commandments. And this is the law and the prophets, for they truly testified of me. (3 Ne. 15:2–10; emphasis added)

THE LORD'S SUPPER

The sacrament is sometimes referred to as the Lord's Supper. The symbolic use of bread and wine is central to its message and similitude. The introduction of the sacrament to the disciples in the upper room is often referred to as the Last Supper. It was a last occasion in the sense that it was the last gathering and instruction of the Twelve prior to the crucifixion. But as a sacrament, it was the "First Supper," the introduction of a new remembrance of him. This act was symbolically a first and last, an "Alpha and Omega" symbolism explored more extensively in chapter 7.

The sacrament itself also foreshadows the supper of the Bridegroom—an event that will be held at the final day. This is the banquet referred to in the parable of the ten virgins. I will not recount this parable again here except to point out that many of the elements of symbolism employed at this last and great banquet are the common symbols used by the Lord in His teaching. The more common and inclusive elements are *bread, wine, oil, light,* and the *Lamb.* Those attending this marriage banquet of the Lord's Supper will include "all the saints," the true shepherds of Israel, they whom the Savior described as "the salt of the earth."

CHAPTER 2
Water

"And the Lord shall guide thee continually, and satisfy thy
soul in drought, and make fat thy bones: and thou shalt be
like a watered garden, and like a spring of water, whose waters
fail not."

—Isaiah 58:11

SHE TRIED TO STAY IN THE SHADOWS AS SHE WALKED THE
nearly deserted streets of Sychar. It was nearing the sixth
hour, and the sun was high and bright in a cloudless sky. The
day was hot and the shade thin along the edges of the one-
story stone shops and homes. Most people stayed inside to
keep out of the midday heat. Perhaps she should have waited
to gather water till evening when the shadows were long and
the temperatures cooler, but for her the heat was preferable
to facing the stares and gossip of the other women who came
morning and evening to Jacob's well.

Life was difficult for any woman in Samaria but especially
hard for an unwed woman. Admittedly, life was better now
than it had been when she was alone, but her neighbors still
didn't approve of her or her family's colorful history. She had
lost or left many men and was just grateful now to have some-
one to look after her. Her trials had slowly softened her over

the years. She was less proud, less judgmental. She had become quick to forgive and sought opportunities to help others whenever she could. She noticed she was more grateful for the little things: the daily walk to get water, anyone who would talk with her, her faith in God, or a quiet moment to pray. She found herself praying more frequently, thanking God for His tender mercies in her life.

She shifted her skin water pot to the other hip as she moved from the side of one building to another. The thought occurred to her that through all her trials, God was aware of her somehow, and loved her; for now, that was enough.

It was not far now, just around the next corner. She was thankful for the short walk to the well and the dependability of the ancient source of water. Father Jacob had dug the well deep enough to sustain life through seasons of drought. Sharing water and preparing a simple meal made her feel useful and needed. It was a blessing to be needed. She just wished she could do more.

Jesus and His disciples had recently been in Judea teaching and "baptizing all people who came unto him" (John 3:22–26). His following and influence were growing (John 3:30). "When therefore the Pharisees had heard that Jesus made and baptized more disciples than John, They sought more diligently some means that they might put him to death. . . . Now the Lord knew this. . . . and he left Judea and departed again into Galilee" (JST, John 4:1–3).

There were three possible routes from Jerusalem and Judea in the south to the Galilee in the north. The easiest was to

depart through the Susa Gate, descend the mountains east-
ward, travel through the Judean wilderness to the ancient city
of Jericho, then follow the fertile Jordan River valley north to
the southern shore of the Sea of Galilee. The most scenic and
interesting route was to take the Joffa road west from Jerusalem
descending down the broad coastal plain to the Mediterranean
Sea. Then, turning north, follow the seashore north past the
Roman resort city of Caesarea to just south of Mount Carmel,
then turn northeast to travel through Megiddo and Nazareth
to the western shore of the Sea of Galilee. The third route was
the middle course—the shortest, most difficult, and most
dangerous. It departed north from Jerusalem through the
Damascus Gate and wound through the rocky highlands of
Samaria to Nazareth and the Galilee beyond. (Note: In the
meridian of time, Samaria was the name of the whole central
region of what today is part of the disputed west bank of the
State of Israel or Palestine.)

The Samaritans were "the people who inhabited Samaria
after the captivity of the northern kingdom of Israel [by
Assyria in 722 BC]. They were the descendants of foreign col-
onists placed there by the Kings of Assyria and Babylonia (2
Kgs. 17:24; Ezra 4:2, 10) [and] Israelites who escaped at the
time of [their] captivity. The population was therefore partly
Israelite and partly gentile. Their religion was also of a mixed
character."[4] As a nation, they possessed the land given to
Joseph's descendants, and they claimed to have helped rebuild
the Jerubbabel Temple in Jerusalem. They recognized Jacob
as their father and maintained that they were inheritors of

the blessing of Abraham through their parentage. The Jews rejected their claims and forbid them to worship at the temple mount. "Their religion, partially pagan in nature, accepted the Pentateuch [the five books of Moses], but rejected the prophets and the psalms. In the day of Jesus they were friendly to Herod and Rome, but bitter toward the Jews, a feeling fully reciprocated by their Jewish kindred."[5]

Given the difficulty of the journey and the state and strength of feelings between these two peoples, it was quite surprising when Jesus "said unto his disciples, *I must needs go through Samaria*" (JST, John 4:6; emphasis added). What was so compelling, so important that He would choose to travel through this difficult and controversial area? His disciples didn't understand but soon would learn the wisdom of His decision as they traveled the rugged mountainous region of central Israel.

"Then he cometh to the city of Samaria, which is called Sychar, near to the parcel of ground which Jacob gave to his son Joseph; the place where Jacob's well was. Now Jesus being weary with the journey, it being about the sixth hour, sat down on the well" (JST, John 4:8).

Turning the last corner, the Samaritan woman saw a strange man sitting near the well, the sun beating on Him mercilessly. As she approached, she was stunned to discover that He was a Jew! What was a Jew doing in the noonday sun in the middle of Samaria? She was so shocked she didn't know what to say, and yet He was positioned such that she couldn't ignore Him as she approached the well.

"And there came a woman of Samaria to draw water; Jesus said unto her, Give me to drink" (JST, John 4:9).

It wasn't proper to address an unknown man in public—especially a Jew! But He was so unusual, and she was curious, so she answered Him, "How is it that thou being a Jew askest drink of me, who am a woman of Samaria? The Jews have no dealings with the Samaritans" (JST, John 4:11).

The next few minutes of conversation would change her life forever. The Savior had initiated the conversation with a request of her, "Give me to drink," knowing it would lead to a discussion. What did He want to discuss with her? What was His divine purpose with this woman?

"Jesus answered and said unto her, If thou knewest the gift of God, and who it is that saith to thee, Give me to drink; thou wouldest have asked of him, and he would have given thee *living water*" (John 4:10; emphasis added).

> Here we view one of the most human scenes of the Master's whole ministry. The Lord of heaven, who created and controls all things, having made clay his tabernacle, [was] physically tired, weary, hungry, and thirsty, following his long journey from Judea. He who had power to draw food and drink from the elements . . . sought rest and refreshment at Jacob's well. In all things he was subjecting himself to the proper experiences of mortality. . . . How graphically Jesus uses the simple truths of everyday life [the need for water] to teach the eternal spiritual realities of his gospel. For the thirsty and choking traveler in a desert wilderness to find water, is to find life.[6]

The woman understood that water was essential for life. That was why she came daily to the well. Is that what He meant by *living* water? She was confused. "The woman saith unto him, Sir, thou hast nothing to draw with, and the well is deep: from whence then hast thou that living water?" (John 4:11). Or was He talking about something else? Who did this man think He was that He could offer something more valuable than the precious water from this historic well? "Art thou greater than our father Jacob, which gave us the well, and drank thereof himself, and his children, and his cattle?" (John 4:12).

Her statement was both a question and a challenge! His answer—divine declaration! Jesus said, "Whosoever drinketh of *this water* shall thirst again: But whosoever drinketh of the water that I shall give him shall never thirst; but the *water that I shall give him* shall be in him a *well of water* springing up into everlasting life" (John 4:13–14; emphasis added).

What was the living water that Jesus offered?

> During His ministry did he just go around doing good, healing the sick, and proclaiming various ethical principles, which if accepted would raise men to a higher way of life? [Teachings of this type are a common sectarian view.] In reality, Jesus taught the gospel of the kingdom of God. That is, he taught that the kingdom of God, which is the Church of Jesus Christ, had again been set up on earth, [as it had been revealed in past dispensations] and that it was the only true and living Church upon the face of the whole earth. He taught the gospel, which means that He taught the terms

and provisions of the plan of salvation. He taught that gospel which embraces all of the laws, principles, doctrines, rites, ordinances, acts, powers, authorities, and keys necessary to save and exalt men in the highest heaven hereafter.

He taught that the gospel or plan of salvation was being restored in His day, so that if men would believe and obey, they could gain peace in this life and eternal life in the world to come. He taught exactly, precisely and identically what he has told the Elders of Israel to teach in [our] day.[7]

He would proclaim, again and again, in plain language that he, Jesus of Nazareth, was the Messiah, the King of Israel, the Son of God, the Redeemer of the world, and the Mediator of the new and everlasting covenant. This was His message. This was His divine declaration. This was His life, mission, and ministry to Samaria. He was and is the author of salvation, the life-giving, life-saving well of water to a barren and desolate world. As water in the desert is life to the weary traveler, Jesus having life in Himself is the giver of life, the Living Water, to all who receive Him and keep His commandments. To Joseph Smith He said, "But unto him that keepeth my commandments I will give the mysteries of my kingdom, and the same shall be in him a well of living water, springing up unto everlasting life" (D&C 63:23; emphasis added).

This is what He was promising the woman at the well! Again He said, "Whosoever drinketh of the water that I shall give him [whoever accepts the sacrifice I will give for him] shall never thirst; but the water that I shall give him [my atonement and the fulness (mysteries) of my gospel] shall be in him a well of water springing up into everlasting life [exaltation in the celestial kingdom of my Father]" (John 4:14; explanation added).

The woman, still confused about the difference between spiritual and temporal blessings, "saith unto him, Sir, give me this water, that I thirst not, neither come hither to draw" (John 4:15).

The Savior knew her situation, her history, and her humility. He had recently met with Nicodemus, a prominent and educated leader of the Jews. What a contrast this woman was to him! This meeting was also a contrast to that one. This uneducated, common woman was willing to talk to Him, a Jew, directly in the full light of day. In contrast, Nicodemus came at night, in secret, to ask his questions. Nicodemus had much to lose as a leader of the Jews. This woman had already lost much. Would she hold anything back? Was she humble enough to accept his word and his word alone? Nicodemus came because of the miracles he had observed, but still he hesitated. This woman had not seen any miracles—would she believe? The Savior now provided her an opportunity to demonstrate her humility by asking a simple direct question: "Jesus saith unto her, Go, call thy husband, and come hither" (John 4:16). The woman, holding nothing back, answered truthfully, saying, "I have no husband." Gently, kindly, Jesus said unto her, "Thou hast well said, I have no husband: For thou hast had five husbands; and he whom thou now hast is not thy husband: in that saidst thou truly" (John 4:17–18).

She had passed a simple test! The Lord had asked an

embarrassing, potentially humiliating, question, especially coming from a stranger, a man, and a Jew! Her answer was direct and honest, open and humble. Even in her ignorance and confusion, the pilot light of faith burned inside her.

"The woman saith unto him, Sir, I perceive that thou art a prophet" (John 4: 19). She had been taught by her fathers here in the shadow of Mount Gerizim that Christ the Messiah would come. Her faith was to follow Him who would be "like unto Moses." She felt compelled to proclaim her simple belief and faith to this extraordinary Jewish man, so "the woman saith unto him, I know that Messias cometh, which is called Christ: when he is come, he will tell us all things." What a joyous event for the Savior! To hear a simple declaration of faith from a humbled woman who knew not that He was the very Christ. With the sun at its apex of light, "Jesus saith unto her, I that speak unto thee am he." Or in other words, "I AM speaketh to thee"! (John 4:26).

This obscure and unknown woman of Samaria was the first person identified in the Gospels to hear the Messiah testify plainly of Himself. Unlike the Jewish leaders in Jerusalem, the woman believed Him and acted on her belief. She disregarded her worldly concerns and straightway "left her waterpot, and went her way into the city, and saith to the men, Come, see a man, which told me all things that ever I did: is not this the Christ? Then they [a multitude] went out of the city, and came unto him" (John 4:28–30). She had herself become a vessel of water, a well of testimony and missionary zeal, a source of living water, springing to action as she shared her personal witness and carried the gospel (good news) to her people. She apparently forgot all about her past history and reputation among the Samaritan community and lost herself in the work of sharing her witness.

His disciples, returning from purchasing food in the Samaritan market, "marveled that he talked with the woman" (John 4:27). As she departed on her personal mission, the Savior turned to His disciples to instruct them. He had just dispatched a humble woman to declare her witness to the Samaritans. In retrospect, His special witnesses may have felt a gentle rebuke as she returned to the very village they had just visited to proclaim the Christ. "Though weary and hungry Jesus' first concern was to plant the seeds of salvation in the hearts of the [soon to be] approaching multitude. Similarly, those sent forth by him to preach the gospel, who have the spirit of their calling, are so imbued with divine zeal that they scarcely take time to eat or rest as they herald the message of salvation to the world."[8]

The Savior said unto them as they pressed Him to eat, "I have meat to eat that ye know not of. . . . My meat is to do the will of him that sent me, and to finish his work" (John 4:32, 34). What is the Father's work? To harvest souls! (See the commentary on Moses 1:39 in chapter 4) Apparently it was middle to late June, far from the traditional harvest time in the fall, but "Jesus saith unto them, Say not ye, There are yet four months, and *then* cometh [the] harvest? behold, I say unto you, Lift up your eyes, and look on the fields; for they are white already to harvest" (John 4:35; D&C 4). Whenever the

Church and kingdom of God is present on earth, we find an extensive emphasis on missionary labors and gospel teaching.

Jesus was in Samaria because of the faith of a woman and others who were prepared to hear and accept His message of the kingdom. He had come to tend and water His garden. The Samaritans had the words of the prophets, and they taught and believed in the Christ. But like some sectarian Christians, they selected what they would believe and worshiped an unknown God, with incomprehensible creeds lacking "body, parts, or passions." As the Lord said to them, "Ye worship ye know not what" (John 4:22).

Christ had come inviting all to come to the waters of baptism so they could come forth from the water spiritually and symbolically washed, sanctified through the blood sacrifice of the Savior and justified by the holy spirit of promise.

> Inasmuch as ye were born into the world by water, and blood, and the spirit, which I have made, and so became of dust a living soul, even so ye must be born again into the kingdom of heaven, of water, and of the Spirit, and be cleansed by blood, even the blood of mine Only Begotten; that ye might be sanctified from all sin, and enjoy the words of eternal life in this world, and eternal life in the world to come, even immortal glory; for by the water ye keep the commandment; by the Spirit ye are justified, and by the blood ye are sanctified. . . . And now, behold, I say unto you: This is the plan of salvation unto all men, through the blood of mine Only Begotten, who shall come in the meridian of time. (Moses 6:59–60, 62)

He came in the meridian of time, He came for us, He

came to Samaria, and He came to a humble woman to declare that He was Living Water.

What were the fruits of the watered garden in Samaria and of the woman's mission and testimony? "Many of the Samaritans of that city believed on [Christ] for the saying of the woman, which testified. . . . So when the Samaritans were come unto him, they besought him that He would tarry with them. . . . And many more believed because of his own word; and said unto the woman, Now we believe . . . and know that this is indeed the Christ, the Saviour of the world" (John 4:39–42).

This "full of faith" woman of Samaria had received Him, the Living Water. She could testify as Isaiah had over 700 years before, "Behold, God is my salvation. . . for the Lord Jehovah is my strength and . . . He also is become my salvation. Therefore with joy shall ye draw water out of the wells of salvation . . . [and] declare his doings among the people . . . for great is the Holy One of Israel in the midst of thee" (Isaiah 12:2–4, 6).

The Savior was indeed in their midst. As the Samaritans came to Him, they requested that He tarry with them; as a result, He abode there two days, after which He departed and continued His journey to the Galilee (John 4:40, 43).

The promise of the Savior to the woman at the well is the same promise we have received in this final dispensation: "If thou shalt ask, thou shalt receive revelation upon revelation, knowledge upon knowledge, that thou mayest know the mysteries and peaceable things—that which bringeth joy, that which bringeth life eternal" (D&C 42:61).

The mysteries of the kingdom are the fulness of the gospel, which can only be received through the keys of the Melchizedek Priesthood and by revelation. "And this greater priesthood administereth the gospel and holdeth the key of the mysteries of the kingdom, even the key of the knowledge of God. Therefore, in the ordinances thereof, the power of godliness is manifest. And without the ordinances thereof, and the authority of the priesthood, the power of godliness is not manifest unto men in the flesh" (D&C 84:19–21).

The first ordinance is the water ordinance of baptism. In the higher ordinances of the temple and through the exercise of Melchizedek Priesthood keys, we receive the mysteries of the kingdom of heaven, we have the heavens opened to us, we commune with the general assembly and Church of the Firstborn, and we enjoy the communion and presence of God the Father and Jesus Christ, the mediator of the new covenant (D&C 107:18–19).

Is not Christ, this well of water, the greatest of all the gifts of God? If found in us, a personal well of water, springing up to everlasting life? As His vessels, we carry the good news of His gospel to the dry and parched gardens of the Lord. For the thirsty and choking traveler in a desert wilderness, to find water is to find life. To the people of Samaria, a humble woman found the fountain of Living Water and carried the blessing of salvation and eternal life to her people, declaring her testimony and losing herself in the work of the Messiah.

How long we have wandered as
strangers in sin,
And cried in the desert for thee!
Our foes have rejoiced,
When our sorrows they're seen,
But Israel will shortly be free.

"Redeemer of Israel," Hymns, no. 6, verse 3.

Commentary

WATER AS A SYMBOL OF LIFE

Water is a symbol of Jesus Christ. He is the Gift of God, the Well of Water, the Spring of Water, the Watered Garden, and the Fountain of Living Water. All these are symbolic expressions of life. He has life in Himself and gives life (resurrection) to all who have ever lived on earth and eternal life (exaltation) to all who repent and come unto Him, enduring to the end. The scriptures declare, "I will pour water upon him that is thirsty, and floods upon the dry ground: I will pour my spirit upon thy seed, and my blessing upon thine offspring. . . . Ho, every one that thirsteth, come ye to the waters" (Isa. 44:3; 55:1). "Yea, come unto Christ, and be perfected in him, and deny yourselves of all ungodliness; and if ye shall deny yourselves of all ungodliness, and love God with all your might, mind and strength, then is his grace sufficient for you. . . that ye become holy, without spot" (Moro. 10:32–33).

A TESTIMONY OF MISSIONARY WORK

This chapter on living water is a testimony of missionary work and the direct and personal involvement of the Savior in the work of the ministry in all lands, among all peoples, and upon all worlds. It also provides insight into the importance of individuals and the impact each of us may have as a missionary of The Church of Jesus Christ of Latter-day Saints if we answer His call to serve.

The story of the woman at the well demonstrates the influence that one member, one conversation, or one discussion can have on the Savior's work. In our daily walk, we can share the true nature of the Father and the Son, the need for continuing revelation and modern prophets, the restoration of the priesthood, the Book of Mormon, the organization of the Church of Jesus Christ, the eternal nature of the family, or the gift of the Holy Ghost.

This event in the Savior's life and ministry demonstrates that Jesus taught the same truths we teach today. He taught the gospel of the kingdom of God. He taught that the kingdom of God had again been set up on earth and that it was the only true and living Church. He taught the terms and provisions of the plan of salvation. He taught and testified that He was the Son of God, the Savior of the world, the one chosen from the beginning to offer a divine sacrifice to answer the demands of justice and to fulfill the plan of the Father in all things. His gospel "embraces all the laws, principles, doctrines, rites, ordinances, acts, powers, authorities, and keys necessary to save and exalt men in the highest heaven hereafter."[9] We also see in His ministry to Samaria a pattern of organization and preparation. From John's Gospel we miss the detail of what He taught, promised, or organized over the two days He remained among the Samaritans, but we see from subsequent events that "the people of Samaria were included among those to whom the apostles were directed to preach the gospel (Acts 1:8), and a very successful work was done there by Philip (Acts 8:4–12)."[10]

It is interesting to note some similarities between the mission to Samaria and the work of the Savior in organizing the future missionary effort in the world of the spirits as recorded in section 138 of the Doctrine and Covenants:

> While this vast multitude waited and conversed, rejoicing in the hour of their deliverance from the chains of death, the Son of God appeared, declaring liberty to the captives who had been faithful; and there He preached to them the everlasting gospel, the doctrine of the resurrection and the redemption of mankind from the fall, and from individual sins on conditions of repentance. . . . But behold, from among the righteous, He organized his forces and appointed messengers, clothed with power and authority, and commissioned them to go forth and carry the light of the gospel to them that were in darkness, even to all the spirits of men; and thus was the gospel preached. (verses 18–19, 30)

It appears that the Lord visited the more humble among the Samaritans and taught the gospel of faith and repentance. He did not, however, go among all the people but organized his followers for future teaching to be directed by His Apostles. He devoted time to teaching these early Samaritan converts, and, as a consequence of his ministry there, He provided personal witnesses from among the Samaritan people who could testify of the Lord in subsequent missions to Samaria. How blessed the woman of Samaria must have felt to be a part of the Lord's early work among her people as she partook of living water and shared her witness of the Messiah.

THE SAVIOR IS INCLUSIVE

The area of Samaria in the meridian of time is now the central region of the modern state of Israel and includes a large part of the contested lands referred to as the West Bank. The modern relationship between the Palestinians and gathering Judah retains the flavor and tenor of the relationship between the Jews and the Samaritans during Christ's ministry. During a business trip to Jerusalem, I attended church at BYU's Jerusalem Center. At that time, the center was not holding classes for study abroad students because of the difficulties between the Jews and the Palestinians (the second intifada). The Jerusalem Center director and his companion were there, as well as a small group of Canadian Saints on tour. Also in attendance were the district president, a missionary couple, and a Palestinian woman from Bethlehem—about fourteen souls altogether. The Palestinian woman was the only Saint in attendance who was not a temporary visitor or a missionary. This woman would rise early each Sabbath morning and travel from Bethlehem in the Palestinian-controlled West Bank, passing through the Israeli security checkpoints, to attend church. Often time it would take three to four hours, and sometimes she was not allowed to pass or attend at all. As I observed her quiet devotion and sensed her testimony and spirit, I thought of the woman of Samaria and her desire to follow the Savior and do what she could to live the truths she was taught.

The only solution to the troubles and conflicts we face is

to have faith in and a testimony of the God of this world, who is Jesus Christ. The resolution to the conflicts between peoples, whether Nephite and Lamanite, Jew and Palestinian, or Samaritan and Gentile is the gospel of Jesus Christ and His atoning sacrifice. In modern Israel, the Jews are witnesses to the promised gathering foretold by ancient and modern prophets. The Lord loves them and will yet remember his promises to Abraham's seed. He no less loves his Palestinian children. Anyone who has felt their friendship, experienced their hospitality, become acquainted with their culture, or witnessed their close-knit families knows of the love the Savior has for them. They too will come to the knowledge of the Lord in the last day and receive the full blessings of the Atonement if they but place their full faith in Him.

SYMBOLISM OF LIGHT

"Say not ye, There are yet four months, and *then* cometh harvest?" (John 4:35). This question implies that the encounter between Jesus and the woman of Samaria took place in late spring or early summer. If his meeting with the woman took place on the summer solstice (June 21) at the sixth hour (noon), that would have been the exact time of the year, in fact the only time of *any* year, to observe the maximum amount of light, the high point of the sun's path in the sky in the Northern Hemisphere—at noon of the longest day of the year. How appropriate it would have been for the Savior, the light of the world, to reveal Himself at this exact time to the woman of Samaria.

PROCLAIMING THE GOSPEL

Opportunities to share the gospel occur everyday. Even though we do not share our Savior's perfection, He remains our standard, our guide, our perfect example of missionary work. We can share the gospel by looking for opportunities to engage others in a gospel discussion. If we do not, we lose the opportunity forever:

Two strangers meet on a dusty road,
Their paths crossing, perhaps only once.
Will they engage one another in a greeting?
Will they be ever better for their meeting?
Or will they let it pass?
A choice opportunity to share the Word,
Along the way . . .

The story of the woman of Samaria is a treasure. The Word shared was living water to the woman and to the Samaritan community. It is the insight of John's Gospel that provides us with this story of living water, a witness to his life, work, and missionary ministry among the Samaritans.

CHAPTER 3
Bread

"And he took bread, and gave thanks, and brake it, and gave unto them, saying, This is my body which is given for you: this do in remembrance of me."

—Luke 22:19

SIMON PETER LAY DOWN TO EAT "AT BREAD," RECLINING IN the traditional pattern of the time. He was thinking about the day's many activities. It had been several years since the Master had charged the twelve to "go ye into all the world, and preach the gospel to every creature" (Mark 16:15). As he pondered, his attention and thoughts were drawn to the small round loaves of bread in the basket. Light from a burning olive oil lamp illuminated the simple room where a few brethren had gathered for evening supper. It was the presence of the bread that caused his mind to wander. He thought about the ways the Lord had used eating and drinking as metaphors for receiving spiritual blessings. Such parabolic symbolism was commonly used among the Jews in teaching, especially with food and drink. The Savior had often used bread to teach and testify of Himself. How could Peter ever look at a loaf of bread or a field of grain again and not think of his Master? How many loaves were there in the basket? There were five! He smiled as his thoughts drifted back to their early days together in the Galilee.

He remembered the Lord praying, "Give us this day our daily bread." He now understood that it was Jesus, the premortal Messiah, who provided the daily manna to his ancestors in the wilderness of Sinai. Many Israelites in the camp mistakenly looked to Moses as the provider of their daily miracle. The Lord's manna was not just provided to sustain their lives but was given as a symbol of the great giver of life. "Manna, or 'Man hu' translated meant, 'What is it' . . . for [the people of Israel] wist not what it was."[11]

In the centuries since Sinai,

> many traditions [were] gathered about the [manna] incident, and were transmitted with invented additions from generation to generation. In the time of Christ the rabbinical teaching was that the manna on which the fathers had fed was literally the food of the angels, sent down from heaven; and that it was of diverse taste and flavor to suit all ages, conditions, or desires; to one it tasted like honey, to another as bread, etc; but in all gentile mouths it was bitter. Moreover it was said that the Messiah would give an unfailing supply of manna to Israel when he came amongst them.[12]

No wonder many of the early followers were confused and had false expectations as they witnessed the miracle of the barley loaves and fishes. Peter remembered the large crowds in Galilee: "And a great multitude followed him, because they saw his miracles which he did on them that were diseased. . . . When Jesus then lifted up *his* eyes, and saw a great company come unto him, he saith unto Philip, Whence shall we buy bread, that these may eat?" Peter now understood that the Master asked this type of question to teach and train the twelve, "for the Lord had already determined as to what was to be done."[13]

"Philip answered him, Two hundred pennyworth of bread is not sufficient for them, that every one of them may take a little. One of his disciples, Andrew, Simon Peter's brother, saith unto him, There is a lad here, which hath five barley loaves, and two small fishes: but what are they among so many?" (John 6:7–9).

Then Jesus made the men sit down in the grass in an orderly manner. They were in number about five thousand men, not including the women and children. "And Jesus took the loaves; and when he had given thanks, he distributed to the disciples, and the disciples to them that were set down; and likewise of the fishes as much as they would" (John 6:11). The substance of the loaves and fishes, the quantitative abundance of bread, increased under the Master's hand! It was bread from Bread!

The Lord then directed that the fragments be gathered up "that nothing be lost" (John 6:12). "The fare was simple, yet . . . satisfying. Barley bread and fish constituted the usual food of the poorer classes of the region."[14] But this meal was anything but usual. The multitude was caught up in the excitement and spectacle of the moment. The people were from all walks of life, and many were there to see miracles and to witness great signs. Some came to see a prophet "like unto Moses" (Acts 3:22). A few knew, even then, that Jesus was the Messiah and would follow Him to their graves. After the miraculous feeding, the multitude agreed that "this is of a truth that prophet that should come into the world" (John 6:14). In their zealous excitement, some tried to proclaim Him King and compel Him to be their leader. Others were looking for a miracle that would surpass their traditions of daily manna and "prove" that He was the promised Messiah, and then there were those who would eventually reject Him, even one from among the Twelve.

During the night, the Apostles and later Jesus crossed over the Sea of Tiberias to Peter's fishing village on the northern shore of Galilee. Peter recalled that the masses from the previous day followed after Him:

> And when they had found him on the other side of the sea, they said unto him, Rabbi, how camest thou here? Jesus answered them and said, Verily, verily, I say unto you, Ye seek me, not because ye desire to keep my sayings, neither because ye saw the miracles, but because ye did eat of the loaves, and were filled. Labour not for the meat which perisheth, but for that meat which endureth unto everlasting life, which the Son of man hath power to give unto you: for him hath God the Father sealed. (JST, John 6:25–27)

His language was clear. His words rebuked their preoccupation with bread and fish and other worldly concerns that perish. Even given the miracle they had just witnessed they sought from Him even greater signs. They reasoned that Moses had given them daily "heavenly" bread, but yesterday they had received only "common" barley loaves. "They said therefore unto him, what sign shewest thou then, that we may see, and believe thee? What dost thou work? Our fathers did eat manna in the desert; as it is written, He gave them bread from heaven to eat" (John 6:30–31). Apparently, the miracle of feeding thousands from five common loaves was not sufficient! As is the case with sign seekers, they sought ever-greater proof.

But Jesus was the bread from heaven and the *bread of heaven*. He was the bread of life, the true living bread, the very staff of life. He was the giver of the law, the great I AM. "Then Jesus said unto them, verily, verily, I say unto you, Moses gave you not that bread from heaven; but my Father giveth you the true bread from heaven. For the bread of God is he which cometh down from heaven, and giveth life unto the world . . . *I am the bread of life*: he that cometh to me shall never hunger" (John 6:32–33, 35; emphasis added).

John the Baptist had previously prophesied, "One mightier than I cometh, the latchet of whose shoes I am not worthy to unloose: he shall baptize you with the Holy Ghost and with fire: Whose fan is in his hand, and he will thoroughly purge his floor, and will gather the wheat into his garner; but the chaff he will burn with fire unquenchable" (Luke 3:16–17). The Lord will test us. He will feel after us. He commands us to come out of the world, "Go ye out from among the nations, even from Babylon, from the midst of wickedness, which is spiritual Babylon" (D&C 133:14). The Lord would soon "purge his threshing floor" by pressing the zealous followers in Capernaum with "hard words"—separating the wheat from the chaff, the sheep from the goats, the seekers of Bread from the seekers of signs.

The Jews then murmured at him, because he said, I am the bread which came down from heaven. And they said, Is not this Jesus, the son of Joseph, whose father and mother we know? How is it then that he saith, I came down from heaven? Jesus therefore answered and said unto them, Murmur not among yourselves. No man can come to me, except he doeth the will of my Father who hath sent me, And this is the will of him who sent me, that ye receive thy Son; for the Father beareth record of him; and he who receiveth the testimony, and doeth the will of him who sent me, I will raise him up in the resurrection of the just. . . . He that believeth on me hath everlasting life. *I am that bread of life.* Your fathers did eat manna in the wilderness, and are dead. This is the bread which cometh down from heaven, that a man may eat thereof, and not die. But *I am the living bread* which came down from heaven: if any man eat of this bread, he shall live for ever: and the bread that I will give *is my flesh*, which I will give for the life of the world. The Jews therefore strove among themselves, saying, How can this man give us *his* flesh to eat? Then Jesus said unto them, verily, verily, I say unto you, Except ye eat the flesh of the Son of man, and drink his blood, ye have no life [faith] in you. . . . Whoso eateth my flesh, and drinketh my blood, [anyone who will make and keep my father's sacred covenants] hath eternal life; and I will raise him up [through the power of my Atonement] in the resurrection of the just at the last day; For my flesh [my offering as a sacrifice] is meat indeed, and [the voluntary shedding of] my blood is drink indeed. (JST, John 6:41–44, 47–55; explanation and emphasis added)

There was little excuse for the Jews pretending to understand that our Lord meant an actual eating and drinking of His material flesh and blood. The utterances to which they objected were far more readily understood by them than they are by us on first reading; for the representations of the law and of truth in general as bread, and the acceptance thereof as a process of eating and drinking, were figures in everyday use by the rabbis of that time. Their failure to comprehend the symbolism of Christ's doctrine was an act of will, not the natural consequence of innocent ignorance.[15]

"These things said he in the synagogue, as he taught in Capernaum" (John 6:59). A pensive sadness came upon Peter as he thought of Capernaum and how his village had rejected the Savior. Jesus had taught several of His more significant discourses there. Despite His words and miracles among this people, they rejected Him because He was mistakenly labeled as a local figure without special value. This discourse on the bread of life was to be His final teaching in the synagogue at Capernaum. After He finished, the Lord cursed the village: "And thou, Capernaum, which art exalted unto heaven, shall be cast down to hell" (Matthew 11:23).

Sadly, the inhabitants of Capernaum failed to recognize or accept the teachings of the Master. Despite rejection, his teachings endured because of their eternal truth and intrinsic value. If the world respects Christ's moral teachings but rejects Him because He claims to be the Son of God, then they reject the living bread and His eternal blessings of exaltation. Our figurative eating of His flesh and the drinking of His blood (as Peter would learn at the Last Supper) is a symbolic representation of his new and everlasting covenant and our absolute unqualified acknowledgment of our total commitment to follow Him. As we partake, we fully accept Him as the Savior and Redeemer of all mankind, of all flesh, on all the earths of his creation. Worlds without end! (See Isa. 45:7; Eph. 3:21; Alma 13:7; D&C 76:112.)

"Many therefore of his disciples [the multitude], when they had heard this, said, This is an hard saying; who can hear it? . . . Jesus knew in himself that his disciples [followers] murmured at it, he said unto them, Doth this offend you?" (John 6:60–61). Jesus knew the hearts and faith of the people. In fact, "Jesus knew from the beginning who they were that believed not, and who should betray him" (John 6:64). The Jews knew the absolute meaning of His words. They had witnessed His works. They understood that His proclamation of eating bread was a declaration of His Messiahship. His words were not hard; what were hard were many of their hearts.

Faith in God is a spiritual gift. The Lord, the Bread of Heaven, declared this when He said, "And these shall all be taught of God. Every man therefore that hath heard, and hath learned of the Father, cometh unto me" (John 6:45). Elder James E. Talmage explained that

> though within the reach of all who diligently strive to gain it, faith is nevertheless a divine gift, and can be obtained only from God. (Matt. 16:17; John 6:44, 65; Eph. 2:8; 1 Cor. 12:9; Rom. 12:3 Moro. 10:11) As is fitting for so priceless a pearl, it is given to those only who show by their sincerity

that they are worthy of it, and who give promise of abiding by its dictates. Although faith is called the first principle of the gospel of Christ, though it be in fact the foundation of religious life, yet even faith is proceeded by sincerity of disposition and humility of soul, whereby the word of God may make an impression upon the heart (Rom. 10:17). No compulsion is used in bringing men to a knowledge of God; yet, as fast as we open our hearts to the influences of righteousness, the faith that leads to life eternal will be given us of our Father.[16]

Jesus attracts and retains the faithful, those whose desires enable them to receive the gift of faith from the Father. When we are "filled with faith," we are motivated to change, repent, and become baptized; that is, we eat the bread and drink the wine of the new covenant. We eat His flesh and drink His blood metaphorically as we unconditionally accept Him, "eating and drinking" Him fully into our lives. Then, as we come to rely daily on Him as we do daily bread, we receive the abundance of His miracles, the quantity of which is represented by bread and the quality of which is represented by wine (see chapter 1).

As we come unto Christ, He claims us as His own: "as thou hast given him power over all flesh, that he should give eternal life to as many as thou hast given him. And this is life eternal, that they might know thee the only true God, and Jesus Christ, whom thou hast sent" (John 17:2–3; emphasis added).

How can we come to know Him if we refuse his offer of daily bread? He is the Bread of Life. He feeds us with his spirit, He feeds us through his anointed servants, He feeds us by the good word of God (John 5: 39), and He blesses us with tender mercies as we choose Him daily.

Many were called, but few were chosen. "From that time many of his disciples [followers] went back, and walked no more with him. Then said Jesus unto the twelve, Will ye also go away? Then Simon Peter answered him, Lord, to whom shall we go? thou hast the words of eternal life. And we believe and are sure that thou art that Christ, the Son of the living God" (John 6:66–70).

Peter's thoughts drifted back to the present as Andrew passed him the small basket of bread. He smiled and stretched forth his hand, picking up a small loaf. He paused for another brief moment. He smelled its familiar comforting aroma and turned it gently in his hand. Bowing his head, He gave thanks and brake.

It tasted sweet, a bit like honey.

God loved us, so he sent his son,
Christ Jesus, the atoning One.
To show us by the path he trod,
The one and only way to God.
This Sacrament doth represent,
His blood and body for me spent.
Partaking now is deed for word,
That I remember him, my Lord.

"God Loved Us, So He Sent His Son," Hymns,
no. 187, verses 1, 5.

Commentary

FROM SMALL THINGS, GREAT THINGS ARE BROUGHT TO PASS

Regarding the loaves and fishes, Andrew noted, "There is a lad here, which hath five barley loaves, and two small fishes: *but what are they among so many?*" (John 6:9; emphasis added). This comment deserves further consideration. I like to think of an Aaronic Priesthood-age youth offering a pitifully small basket of loaves and fishes. What difference could such a basket make? How insignificant it was compared to the needs and "demands of the world"! Andrew said it well when he observed, "But what are they [we] among so many"? What are we, as members of the Church, as a quorum, a presidency, or a home or visiting teacher among the many who have such great need? All the souls we strive to serve are hungry, and their need is great. How can we hope to satisfy their hunger?

The solution is in the touch of the Master's hand. The miracle of quantitative abundance is multiplicative. The Lord multiplies our effectiveness as we magnify our callings. Any action we take under the direction of the Spirit is sanctified by the Spirit and is enlarged, purified, extended, and expanded by the abundant touch of the Master. The Lord Himself declared:

The weak things of the world shall come forth and break down the mighty and strong ones, that man should not counsel his fellow man, neither trust in the arm of flesh; but that every man might speak in the name of God the Lord, even the

Savior of the world; that faith also might increase in the earth; that mine everlasting covenant might be established; that the fulness of my gospel might be proclaimed by the weak and the simple unto the ends of the world, and before kings and rulers.

Behold, I am God and have spoken it; these commandments are of me, and were given unto my servants in their weakness, after the manner of their language, that they might come to understanding. And inasmuch as they erred it might be made known; and inasmuch as they sought wisdom they might be instructed; and inasmuch as they sinned they might be chastened, that they might repent; and inasmuch as they were humble they might be made strong, and blessed from on high, and receive knowledge from time to time.

And after having received the record of the Nephites, yea, even my servant Joseph Smith, Jun., might have power to translate through the mercy of God, by the power of God, the Book of Mormon. And also those to whom these commandments were given, might have power to lay the foundation of this church, and to bring it forth out of obscurity and out of darkness, the only true and living church upon the face of the whole earth, with which I, the Lord, am well pleased. (D&C 1:19–30)

The Lord supports us and sustains us in everything we undertake in his name that is worthy of Him. The issue is not "What are [we] among so many?" but rather "If the Lord be for us, who may stand against us?" The pinnacle trial of this life is to receive faith in the Lord Jesus Christ and to see if we will put our whole trust in Him. If we do, all things are possible.

TEACHING MOMENTS

The Lord of Heaven is not just a master teacher, He is *the* Master Teacher. An observation of his many, diverse, and symbolic methods exemplify his effectiveness in teaching all types of individuals under various situations. When the Lord fed the five thousand, He created enough bread that "all were filled." In fact, there was bread left over after all had eaten their fill. Surely a God who knows all can estimate food consumption down to the exact morsel, so why did He create more than was needed? Elder Talmage instructed, "Our Lord's direction to gather up the fragments was an impressive object-lesson against waste; and it may have been to afford such lesson that an excess was supplied. The fare was simple, yet satisfying. Barley bread and fish constituted the usual food of the poorer classes of the region." He goes on to point out the different object lessons represented by the bread and wine: "The conversion of water into wine at Cana was a qualitative transmutation; the feeding of the multitude [barley loaves and fishes] involved a quantitative increase; who can say that one, or which, of these miracles of provision was the more wonderful?"[17] In fact, each miracle is a type and similitude of Christ and his attributes: quantity (common bread) and quality (the best wine). Both are a bold statement of the available abundance He offers to each of us.

HARD WORDS

The Lord's work and miracles in all ages attracts the faithful, curious, eccentric, distracters, and opponents. The sermon on the Bread of Life was a time of pruning, separation, and sifting for the crowds in Galilee. Elder Bruce R. McConkie wrote,

> This testing and sifting process has ever been part of the Lord's system. Men have been placed on earth to be tried and tested, 'to see if they will do all things whatsoever the Lord their God shall command them.' (Abraham 3:25) After they accept the gospel and join the Church, this testing process continues, indeed, is often intensified. 'I have decreed in my heart, saith the Lord, that I will prove you in all things, whether you will abide in my covenant, even unto death, that you may be found worthy. For if ye will not abide in my covenant ye are not worthy of me.' (D&C 98:14–15)[18]

Of particular interest in John's commentary is the eventual separation of Judas Iscariot, son of Simon, from the rest of the Twelve. The Bread of Life record in John chapter 6 ends with the foreshadowing exposure of Judas's betrayal: "Jesus answered them, Have not I chosen you twelve, and one of you is a devil? He spake of Judas Iscariot *the son* of Simon: for he it was that should betray him, being one of the twelve" (John 6:70–71).

THE HOUSE OF BREAD

Our Savior would have been commonly known in the meridian of time as Joshua ben Joseph (Jesus the son of Joseph). In reality, He is the only begotten Son of Elohim in the flesh and was born of Miriam (Mary) in Bethlehem, the ancient ancestral village of David. The name *Bethlehem* means "House of Bread." Both Joseph and Mary were direct descendants of King David; as such, Jesus was by both birth and adoption born of King David's royal line. He was literally born King of the Jews, in the house of bread.

THE FEAST OF THE BRIDEGROOM

The sacrament (of the Lord's Supper) prepares us to attend the Lord's final wedding banquet of the Bridegroom when He comes in His glory. In this chapter, I referenced a scripture in the Doctrine and Covenants, which commands us all to "go ye out from among the nations, even from Babylon" (D&C 133:14). The command to "go ye out" from the world is a requirement to attend the Lord's final supper. The imagery of "going out" to be able to "come in" to this supper is a lesson and invitation to become like Him. The message is to "deny [ourselves] of all unrighteousness" by putting our wants and desires last. This going out of Babylon allows us to come in, or as the Savior stated it, the last shall be first and the first shall be the last. The qualification for this last supper with Him is the accomplishment of his command to be perfected in Him by following his example and receiving the "wedding gifts" He offers.

This banquet event is foreshadowed by the sacrament of the Lord's Supper and made possible by the Lord's infinite and eternal Atonement. As separating yourself from the world is required to be accepted at the banquet, the Lord declared in a subsequent verse, "Wherefore, prepare ye for the coming of the Bridegroom; *go ye, go ye out to meet him*" (D&C

133:19; emphasis added). To be invited in to the feast of the Bridegroom, we must choose His kingdom over Babylon. It is at this final supper that the Lord will provide his "unfailing supply of manna to Israel."

CHAPTER 4
Stone

Then, O Rock of our salvation,
Jesus, Savior of the world,
Take us from our lowly station;
Let our flag with thee be furled.

—"O Thou Rock of Our Salvation," *Hymns,* no. 258

SHE SCRAPED HER KNEE WHILE THEY DRAGGED HER UP the stone steps leading to Solomon's Porch. The celebrations of the night before were a fading memory as they approached the temple mount. The scene was odd in several ways. The men who had arrested her were in a hurry and showed no regret for their rough treatment. The officials normally ignored such women, especially this early in the day. Plus, this was the morning after the great feast—usually a time for rest, recuperation, and cleanup. People were whispering, pointing, and beginning to follow behind the gathering crowd, as if they could smell the scent of a public humiliation. One thing was certain—something unusual was developing and no one wanted to miss the spectacle.

The events of the previous week had been the most anticipated of the Jewish year. "The Feast," as it had come to be called, was the Feast of Tabernacles, the last, greatest, and most joyful of the festival season. "The law commanded that three times a year all the males of the covenant people were to appear before the Lord in the place [Jerusalem] that he should choose."[19] This great last feast served as a reminder of the wanderings of the children of Israel in the wilderness and celebrated the gathering of the fruits of the harvest. It was like combining Pioneer Day with the Thanksgiving holiday. The week-long celebration and sacrifices were said to be the most memorable and joyful events of the year. It was held in the fall, usually in September or October, and lasted for seven days. To the seven was added an eighth day, "the last day, that great day of the feast" (John 7:37), "a day of holy convocation, which marked the ending not only of this particular feast, but of the whole festival season."[20]

The Jews came from every part of the land to participate. A few came because of deep faith and obedience. Some came to be taught by rabbis or to discuss the law. Many came because of the spectacle and festivities. The population of Jerusalem would triple as families gathered to pitch tents or make ritual canopies of willows as temporary dwellings.

Merchants also came. These businessmen provided all the goods and services the people needed. They sold food and house-wares, new garments, and items of every shape and kind from their temporary booths. The people were required to wash, put on clean garments, exchange their coins for temple money, purchase sacrifices and present their offerings to the Levite priests as part of their observances and celebration. Most festivalgo-ers would purchase these items in Jerusalem rather than worry about transporting them from their homes. As a consequence, the feast was also big business for the Sanhedrin, who governed Jerusalem under the authority of the Roman procurator of Judea, Pontius Pilate. The Sanhedrin (whose seventy-one aristocratic members included Pharisees, scribes, and Sadducees) jealously guarded their control of the city and the commerce that brought them riches and power. Their control over the temple was used as the symbolic centerpiece of their authority. They selfishly protected their control of both it and the temple mount and rejected any claim to religious authority other than their own. During the Feast of Tabernacles, the temple and the temple mount were a continual scene of activity and spectacle, of observances and profiteering, of faith and faithlessness.

This year, the Sanhedrin was increasingly concerned about a particular problem. A Galilean Rabbi had been stirring up the people with his radical teachings and purported miracles. He had been in Jerusalem not long ago and was expected back this week for the feast. The leaders of the Jews sought an opportunity to confront Him.

Jesus had many followers, and many more were curious about Him, hoping to see this Galilean at the festival. From the establishment's perspective, His growing influence had to be discredited without inciting a riot, an event that would definitely create problems with the Romans. This Jesus would not recognize the authority of the Sanhedrin or the high priest! He claimed divine authority, and His ministry was a serious challenge that, in their view, must be dealt with. "The Jews [the Sanhedrin] sought to kill him" (John 7:1).

Before the feast, Jesus had been in the Galilee with His friends and family, some of whom encouraged Him to go up to Jerusalem for the celebration "that thy [followers] also may see the works that thou doest;. . . if thou do these things, shew thyself to the world" (John 7:3–4). But Jesus replied, "Go ye up unto this feast: I go not up yet unto this feast: for my time is not yet full come" (John 7:8). The Savior did not seek to create a spectacle or to aggrandize Himself with a miraculous public demonstration. But in the end, a miracle is exactly what happened.

His brethren had finally "gone up" to the feast, expecting that Jesus would not attend. But their Master was compelled to go. "Then went he also up unto the feast, not openly, but as it were in secret. Then the Jews sought him at the feast, and said, where is he? And there was much murmuring among the people concerning him" (John 7:10–12). The people were understandably curious. They wanted to see this Galilean of whom they had heard so much. There were many different opinions of Him. Some said He was a good man. Others said He was a deceiver. "So there was a division among the people because of him" (John 7:43). "Howbeit no man spake openly of him for fear of the Jews" (John 7:13).

The festival week started without Jesus. The leaders of the Jews were expecting Him to come for the beginning of the festival. They had issued orders to the officers (temple guards) to take Him, and the people knew the officials were looking for Him. The Savior eventually arrived on about the fourth day and returned again on the last or eighth day to teach on the temple mount. Many were impressed with His words and wondered how He knew so much, "having never learned" (John 7:15). He taught many points of doctrine as one having authority, declaring, "My doctrine is not mine, but his that sent me. If any man will do his will, he shall know of the doctrine, whether it be of God, or whether I speak of myself" (John 7:16–17). The people listening knew He was the man the Sanhedrin was looking for, and they wondered why it was not obvious to the officers. "But no man laid hands on him. Then came the officers to the chief priests and Pharisees; and they said unto them [the officers], Why have ye not brought him? The officers answered, Never [a] man spake like this man" (John 7:44–46).

The Pharisees and scribes of the Sanhedrin were frustrated, fearful, and irate. Jesus was never where they expected Him to be. Just when they thought He was not coming, He appeared. Instead of being confronted and embarrassed in His teaching, He was being recognized as one having authority, drawing away many of the people. His following was growing, His influence was increasing, and the people were all talking, albeit in secret, about Jesus. The Pharisees and the scribes wanted to discredit and embarrass Him, but they thought they had lost their chance! It was now sunset on "the last day, that great day of the feast" (John 7:37). What a wonder this last night was—the highlight of the week's celebration! Tonight brought the illumination of the temple courts by four golden candelabra filled to the brim with olive oil harvested from the Mount of Olives (see chapter 5). It was the pinnacle of the feast and the time for joyous celebration. Many would make merry tonight, but not the scribes or the Pharisees.

The Savior had retired to the Mount of Olives for the evening (see John 8:1). Perhaps He looked down on the temple that night as the fires were lighted and the temple mount was illuminated from the golden glow of the torches. Perhaps He thought of the ingathering of the harvest, the celebrations of gratitude, or the tender mercies the Lord extends to the house of Israel. Perhaps He thought of the sacrifices that had been offered during the week and of the great and last sacrifice that was soon to be made. Perhaps He reflected on the hearts of the people who were wandering in darkness, even as the light of the world walked among them.

Early the next morning, John records, "he came again into the temple, and all the people came unto him; and he sat down and taught them" (John 8:2). Word must have spread quickly to the scribes and Pharisees that Jesus was there. Perhaps it was not too late to discredit and embarrass Him? The plan quickly came together. . . .

No one today knows who this woman was. Was she brought before the Sanhedrin for judgment during the previous night? Was she set up to be betrayed as a pawn in this power struggle? Was she known as an adulteress, or was it a coincidence that she was "caught in the act"? Whatever the circumstances, she became a key figure in this drama to confront and entrap Jesus. As she was dragged to the temple mount to be put on public display, what must she have thought? What was she to endure? Embarrassment, betrayal, humiliation?

How did she feel? Worthless, abandoned, forsaken? Even as she was placed "in the midst of the people," she must have felt terribly alone.

John records, "And the scribes and Pharisees brought unto him a woman taken in adultery; and when they had set her in the midst of the people, They say unto him, Master, this woman was taken in adultery, in the very act. Now Moses in the law commanded us, that such should be stoned; but what sayest thou?" (JST, John 8:3–4).

> Under the law of Moses, adultery was punishable by death (Leviticus 20:10), and stoning was the ordinary means of carrying out the penalty (Exodus 17:4). It was required that the witnesses be the first to cast a stone and afterward all the people (Deut. 13: 9–10; 17: 6–7).
>
> Apparently, at this time the death penalty for adultery was no longer used (John 7: 19–20). Presumably, the people did not want it, and the Roman law did not prescribe it. And in any case, it would require the approval of the Roman authorities. In setting the woman in the midst of the people and asking Jesus this question, the scribes and Pharisees had presumably set up a situation that they felt would trap Jesus into answering one way or another, and therefore they would have something of which to accuse him. If Jesus agreed to stoning, he would be seen as going against the Romans. If he did not agree, he would be seen as going against Moses.[21]

A confrontation had been staged, a challenge given, the law quoted, and the trap set. The Pharisees had presented before the people a public challenge to the authority of Jesus, thus "tempting him, that they might have to accuse him" (John 8:6). The people, followers and skeptics alike, looked to Jesus and awaited His reply.

Upon reflection, it appears the Savior's first concern was not the pressing accusers or the gathered crowd but rather for the nameless woman. Jesus came not to condemn or exploit, but to redeem (see John 3:17). The Savior, and perhaps none other, looked upon the woman with eternal compassion and perspective. Who could know how she felt? Who knew her fears, her embarrassments? Only He who would experience all the pains, sorrows, and grief of the penitent (see Isa. 53:3), He who would claim all those who believe on Him. As He looked upon her, "Jesus stooped down [signifying his condescension] and with his finger wrote on the ground, as though he heard them not" (John 8:6).

The accusers continued to press Jesus for an answer. Perhaps He was thinking of the previous night, east across the Kidron Valley to the Mount of Olives, where He had spent the night. There among the olive tree vineyards; there where in the not-too-distant future, He would ask His disciples to watch and "pray that ye enter not into temptation. And he was withdrawn from them about a stone's cast, and kneeled down and prayed, saying, 'Father, if thou be willing, remove this cup from me: nevertheless not my will, but thine be done.' And being in an agony he prayed more earnestly: and his sweat was as it were great drops of blood falling down to the ground" (Luke 22:40–42, 44; emphasis added).

His central act is the foundation of the Father's plan of

Figure 1–1. *Christ Washing the Disciples' Feet* by Jeffrey Hein.
During the last meeting with His disciples, the Savior observed
the Passover, introduced the sacrament, washed the disciples'
feet, and prayed for them before departing for Gethsemane.

Figure 1–2. Christ's vivid robe in Jeffrey Hein's *As a Hen Gathereth* reminds us of His wine symbolism and His promised return in glory, adorned in red.

Figure 1–3. *Abinadi*, a study by Jeffrey Hein.
Abinadi taught of the Messiah and His fulfillment
of the law of Moses before the court of King Noah.

Figure 2–1. A spring of fresh water near Caesarea Philippi.
Photo by Patti Amacher.

Figure 3–1 *Moses,* a study by Jeffrey Hein.
Moses taught that manna, or heavenly bread,
came from God, the giver of the law and life.

Figure 3–2. *Raising the Daughter of Jarius* by Jeffrey Hein.
Miracles such as raising the daughter of Jarius attracted
the curious and the faithful while in the Galilee.

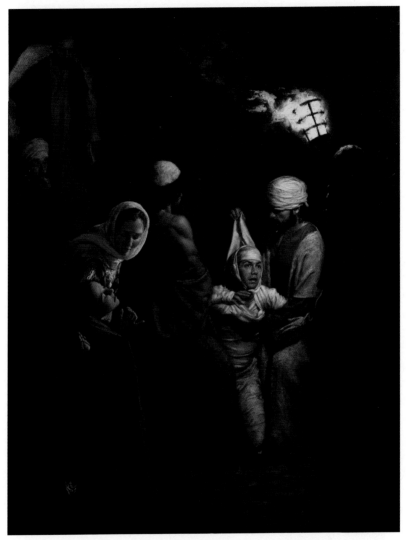

Figure 3–3. *The Raising of Lazarus* by Jeffrey Hein.
The Savior's miracles were also a threat to the power and control of
the Sanhedrin who sought opportunities to accuse this young Rabbi.

Figure 4–1. A secluded spot in the Garden of Gethsemane a "stone's cast away." Photo by Patti Amacher.

Figure 4–2. An outcropping of fractured stone near Liberty, Missouri. Photo by Patti Amacher.

Figure 4–3. *Neither Do I Condemn Thee* by Jeffrey Hein.
Christ taught on the temple mount a lesson on compassion, service, and a
focus on the individual while symbolically representing His life's mission.

Figure 5–1. *Prepared with Oil* by Michael Malm.

Figure 5–2. An aged olive tree in the Garden of
Gethsemane, Mount of Olives, Jerusalem, Israel.
Photo by Patti Amacher.

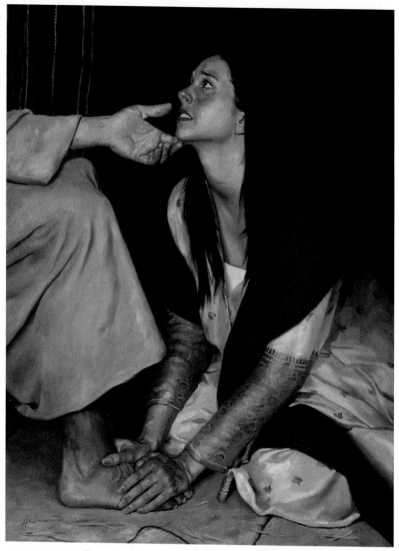

Figure 5–3. *For She Loved Much* by Jeffrey Hein.
Mary demonstrates her love for the Savior during the last week of His mortal ministry.

Figure 5–4. *An Olive Oil Lamp and Light* by Michael Malm.

Figure 6–1. *The Shepherd of the Lord* by Nathan Pinnock.
Spring lambs were raised for centuries in the valleys south of the temple mount
where Abraham and Isaac traveled to obey the Lord's command to offer sacrifice.

Figure 6–2. *Isaac,* a study by Jeffrey Hein.
Isaac submitted his will to his father "even unto death,"
making him a fitting similitude for the Savior.

Figure 7–1. *Ascension in America* by Jeffrey Hein.
"I am the Lord thy God, I am Alpha and Omega."

redemption. Isaiah prophesied, "Therefore thus saith the Lord God, Behold, I lay in Zion for a foundation a stone, a tried stone, a precious corner stone, a sure foundation" (Isa. 28:16; emphasis added). Joseph Smith recorded, "Wherefore, I am in your midst, and I am the good shepherd, and the stone of Israel. He that buildeth upon this rock shall never fail" (D&C 50:44; emphasis added). And regarding the Jews at Jerusalem, Jacob wrote, "And now I, Jacob am led on by the spirit unto prophesying: for I perceive by the workings of the Spirit which is in me, that by the stumbling of the Jews they will reject the stone upon which they might build and have foundation. But behold, according to the scriptures, this stone shall become the great, and the last, and the only sure foundation, upon which the Jews can build" (Jacob 4:15–16; emphasis added).

Looking at the woman and hearing the continued accusations, the Savior of the world "lifted up himself, [symbolic of his power over death] and said unto them, He that is without sin among you [Jesus], let him first cast a stone at her" (John 8:7; emphasis added). Was He simply saying, "Before you condemn her, first offer her the blessings of the holy atonement through him who is without blemish and without spot among you?" He could have said, "I AM before you, the Son of Man, the only sinless person ever to live on the worlds which I, God, have created. I, who will bear the sufferings and pains of all mankind; I, who will withdraw a stone's cast away from my Apostles to drink the bitter cup that my Father hath given me; behold, I offer myself 'a sacrifice for sin, to answer the ends of the law' (see 2 Ne. 2:7) and to satisfy the demands of justice. Before you condemn her, first seek to reclaim her. Cast me at her, the Stone of Israel, the chief cornerstone" (Acts 4:11).

But without confrontation or commentary, the Savior

> again stooped down, and wrote on the ground. And they which heard it, being convicted by their own conscience, went out one by one, beginning at the eldest, even unto the last: and Jesus was left alone, and the woman standing in the midst of the temple. When Jesus had raised up himself, and saw none of her accusers, and the woman standing, he said unto her, Woman, where are those thine accusers? Hath no man condemned thee? She said, No man, Lord. And Jesus said unto her, Neither do I condemn thee: go, and sin no more. And the woman glorified God from that hour, and believed on his name. (JST, John 8:8–11; emphasis added)

We now know the true miracle of that day. "The happy result [was] the harvest of a soul during the Feast of Tabernacles. The woman believed in Jesus Christ. Apparently, her heart was changed from that very hour because of the gentle and compassionate manner in which the master handled this difficult situation"[22]

This great last feast of the festival season reminded the participants of the wanderings of the children of Israel in the wilderness and celebrated the ingathering of the fruits of the year. Ironically, the leaders of the Jews who should have been leading the people to Christ were "wandering in the wilderness." The unknown woman was also lost. But the Savior had come in the meridian of time to fulfill the Atonement, satisfy the demands of justice, and extend mercy "unto all those who have a broken heart and a contrite spirit" (2 Ne. 2:7). He was ingathering a harvest of souls! What is the worth of a soul? As infinite and as significant as the eternal Atonement itself! Every soul harvested gathers in a miracle worthy of thanksgiving.

As the woman walked away in the light of Christ, Jesus said, "I am the light of the world, he that followeth me shall not walk in darkness but shall have the light of life" (John 8:12). Then said Jesus to those Jews who believed on Him: "If ye continue in my word, then are ye my disciples indeed; and ye shall know the truth, and the truth shall make you free" (John 8:31–32).

May each of us share our testimony of Christ, teach repentance, quickly forgive one another, and live to be free from the blood and sins of this generation through the Atonement of our Lord and Savior, Jesus Christ, the Stone of Israel, "a tried stone, a precious corner stone, a sure foundation" (Isa. 28:16).

I stand all amazed at the love Jesus
offers me,
Confused at the grace that so fully he
proffers me.
I tremble to know that for me he was
crucified,
That for me a sinner, he suffered, he bled
and died.
Oh, it is wonderful, that he should care
for me,
Enough to die for me!
Oh, it is wonderful, wonderful to me!

"I Stand All Amazed," Hymns, no. 193,
verse 1.

Commentary

THE JOSEPH SMITH TRANSLATION OF JOHN, CHAPTER 8

Joseph Smith made few changes to the text of John, chapter 8, in his inspired translation. However, three major additions to the King James Version text combine to add clarity, richness, depth of understanding, and focus to this significant event in the Lord's mortal ministry. The additions, in bold, are as follows:

3 And the scribes and Pharisees brought unto him a woman taken in adultery; and when they had set her in the midst **of the people,**

4 They say unto him, Master, this woman was taken in adultery, in the very act.

5 Now Moses in the law commanded us, that such should be stoned: but what sayest thou?

6 This they said, tempting him, that they might have to accuse him. But Jesus stooped down, and with *his* finger wrote on the ground, *as though he heard them not.*

7 So when they continued asking him, he lifted up himself, and said unto them, He that is without sin among you, let him first cast a stone at her.

8 And again he stooped down, and wrote on the ground.

9 And they which heard *it,* being convicted by *their own* conscience, went out one by one, beginning at the eldest, *even* unto the last: and Jesus was left alone, and the woman standing in the midst **of the temple.**

10 When Jesus had lifted up himself, and saw none but the

woman, he said unto her, Woman, where are those thine accusers? hath no man condemned thee?

11 She said, No man, Lord. And Jesus said unto her, Neither do I condemn thee: go, and sin no more. **And the woman glorified God from that hour, and believed on his name** (JST, John 8:3–11).

These corrections reflect the Savior's focus on the condition, state, and redemption of the woman. The first addition in verse 3 indicated her physical location and the intent of her accusers, as well as her orientation to the world—she was "in the midst of the people." In the second addition, verse 9, her relationship and orientation had changed to Christ, "standing in the midst of the temple." The final correction in verse 11 confirms that this was a permanent change and testifies of her conversion "from that hour." From these revelations, we gain insight into the Lord's interest and involvement in individual lives, His concern for the one, and His focus on personal conversion and redemption. He came up to this feast to teach. His most personal lesson was taught by example while reclaiming a woman whom everyone else had abandoned, shunned, ridiculed, exploited, or condemned.

OTHER FOUNDATION STONES

The Lord Jesus Christ is the Stone of Israel. His mortal life and Atonement is the cornerstone of the gospel and the only foundation upon which men may be redeemed from their lost and fallen state in mortality. The use of the stone imagery is often referenced throughout the scriptures. (For example, see

Deut. 32:15; 1 Sam. 2:2; Job 38:6; Ps. 118:22; Matt. 21:42–44; Mark 12:10; Luke 20:17; Acts 4:10–12; Eph. 2:20; 1 Pet. 2:6; Jacob 4:15; Hel. 5:12; D&C 50:44.) In one example, the Lord refers to Peter by his Aramaic name, Cephas, which means "rock" or "little stone." Peter's name reflects his testimony of the Savior as the true keystone of the Church, the source or rock of revelation, and his call as the presiding Apostle and high priest of the ancient church. The Lord calls others to stand with Him in the work in all gospel dispensations. In our latter-day dispensation, for instance, who can doubt that Joseph Smith stands as the foundation of the restoration and one of Christ's "little stones"?

WHERE WAS THE MAN?

The following is an insightful commentary from my brother, Grant, on this chapter: "I had a thought as I read, where was the man? If she were caught in the very act, they should have brought both guilty parties before Christ if they were really interested in justice. The man was most likely at more fault than the woman. . . . Did they only bring the woman because the man was party to the trap, or did they want to play on the sympathies of the crowd? How often women suffer the consequences and public humiliations of immoral behavior while the men recede into the background and refuse to take responsibility.

"Jesus, however, did not concern himself with these obvious lapses of conscience by the accusers, but showed concern for the woman's soul and the administration of the law, with mercy, that He Himself gave to Moses so many years before. How ironic that they would question the author of the law, whose intent was to guide His children to happiness and warn them of the pitfalls of mortality, and then to walk away dejected, when He taught them the true spirit and meaning of His law. As the crowd dispersed, only the woman remained behind to hear what Jesus had to say to her. She was the one who received the greatest blessings taught that day, because she was willing to listen to the Savior and repent of her sins. She heard the Savior say to her, 'Neither do I condemn thee.' How would we know these words if she had not repented 'from that hour and believed on his name,' became a member of His Church, and followed the Savior?"

THE EARTH'S TESTIMONY OF CHRIST

The earth itself proclaims that Christ is the sure foundation, the very Stone of Israel. The Book of Mormon records just prior to the crucifixion,

> But behold, as I said unto you concerning another sign, a sign of his death, behold, in that day that he shall suffer death the sun shall be darkened and refuse to give his light unto you; and also the moon and the stars; and there shall be no light upon the face of this land, even from the time that he shall suffer death, for the space of three days, to the time that he shall rise again from the dead. Yea, at the time that he shall yield up the ghost there shall be thunderings and lightnings for the space of many hours, and the earth shall shake and tremble; and the rocks which are upon the face of this earth,

which are both above the earth and beneath, which ye know at this time are solid, or the more part of it is one solid mass, shall be broken up. (Hel. 14:20–21)

Apparently the physical condition of the earth was different before the Atonement, as witnessed by Nephi, son of Helaman. After the destruction and signs were given, Nephi records, "And thus the face of the whole earth became deformed, because of the tempests, and the thunderings, and the lightnings, and the quaking of the earth. *And behold, the rocks were rent in twain; they were broken up upon the face of the whole earth, insomuch that they were found in broken fragments, and in seams and in cracks, upon all the face of the land*" (3 Nephi 8:18; emphasis added).

The breaking of the rocks signifies the pains and sufferings of its Creator (see 1 Ne. 19: 12) and reverences the true Stone of Israel. They will remain broken until the Lord returns in his glory and heals the earth through the power of the resurrection. In that day, Israel will be gathered, Zion, the new Jerusalem will be built upon the American continent, and Christ will reign personally upon the earth, which will be renewed and receive its paradisiacal glory (Articles of Faith 1:10).

REMEMBERING THE STONE

Parents have a sacred responsibility to teach their children the truths of the gospel. The most important truth and testimony is of the central role of Christ in our lives. In the sacrament, we covenant to "always remember Him." Remembrance is key. Wise parents of all dispensations have taught this to their children and have testified of Him.

Using the stone imagery, Helaman instructed his sons Nephi and Lehi

O remember, remember, my sons, the words which king Benjamin spake unto his people; yea, remember that there is no other way nor means whereby man can be saved, only through the atoning blood of Jesus Christ, who shall come; yea, remember that he cometh to redeem the world. And remember also the words which Amulek spake unto Zeezrom, in the city of Ammonihah; for he said unto him that the Lord surely should come to redeem his people, but that he should not come to redeem them in their sins, but to redeem them from their sins. And he hath power given unto him from the Father to redeem them from their sins because of repentance; therefore he hath sent his angels to declare the tidings of the conditions of repentance, which bringeth unto the power of the Redeemer, unto the salvation of their souls.

And now, my sons, remember, remember that it is upon the rock of our Redeemer, who is Christ, the Son of God, that ye must build your foundation; that when the devil shall send forth his mighty winds, yea, his shafts in the whirlwind, yea, when all his hail and his mighty storm shall beat upon you, it shall have no power over you to drag you down to the gulf of misery and endless wo, *because of the rock upon which ye are built, which is a sure foundation, a foundation whereon if men build they cannot fall.*

And it came to pass that these were the words which Helaman taught to his sons; yea, he did teach them many things which are not written, and also many things which are written. And they did remember his words; and therefore they went forth, keeping the commandments of God, to teach the word of God among all the people of Nephi. (Hel. 5:9–14; emphasis added)

CHAPTER 5
Oil

"And thou shalt command the children of Israel, that they bring thee pure oil olive beaten for the light, to cause the lamp to burn always. . . *it shall be* a statute for ever unto their generations on the behalf of the children of Israel."

—Exodus 27:20–21

THE SAVIOR'S LAST WALK UP FROM JERICHO THROUGH THE Judean wilderness to Bethany was long and exhausting. The path ascended nearly four thousand feet over seventeen difficult miles. Bethany was close to Jerusalem—very close, less than a mile southeast over the Mount of Olives. Bethany was seldom, if ever, frequented by the "elite" of the templed city. It was considered unclean, a place for lepers and castoffs. Still, for Jesus and his followers, it was a quiet and safe place to observe the Sabbath with friends and loved ones. Jesus and his disciples probably arrived at the house of Simon the leper on the Friday before Passover week. As the sun slipped below the western horizon, a waxing moon would soon rise in the east over the Mount of Olives, signifying the approaching Passover and heralding the last Sabbath of the Lord's mortal ministry.

The Lord's sadness was evident. On the journey up from Jericho, He had been solemn and reflective. He had confided with the twelve the reason for his condition, saying, "Behold, we go up to Jerusalem; and the Son of man shall be betrayed unto the chief priests and unto the scribes, and they shall condemn him to death, And shall deliver him to the Gentiles to mock, and to scourge, and to crucify *him:* and the third day he shall rise again" (Matt. 20:18–19). This was apparently His third direct testimony to His disciples of His pending suffering, sacrifice, and resurrection, but it didn't immediately register with the Twelve. They would not or could not comprehend it. The Master had demonstrated so much power since their call to follow Him—He controlled the elements and had power over sickness and death—surely He could do all things. Perhaps they thought He was speaking metaphorically. In any event, they did not comprehend the reality of His declarations.

But there was one among them who understood—she had demonstrated her sensitivity and understanding in the past. She now felt what was about to happen, and she would act. It was Mary, the sister of Martha and Lazarus.

The details of this last intimate Sabbath scene are not fully given in the Gospels, nor have the exact relationships been delineated between the identified participants. Had Simon been healed of his leprosy as Lazarus had been raised from death? Was Simon the father of Mary, Martha, and Lazarus? Was this where they usually stayed while in Bethany? In this regard, we will respect the "reverent curtain" the Gospel authors have drawn over these personal details (as did Joseph Smith Jr. in his inspired translation of the Gospels). It is sufficient for now that we know Jesus passed the day in the home of His friends in reverent observance of the Sabbath.

After Shabbat, as was their custom, they ate: "There they made him a supper; and Martha served. . . . Then took Mary a pound of ointment of spikenard, very costly, and anointed the feet of Jesus, and wiped his feet with her hair: and the house was filled with the odour of the ointment" (John 12:2–3; see also Matt. 26:6–13).

Regarding her act of love, two apostolic scholars have commented:

> To understand this solemn scene one must both know and feel the religious significance of Mary's act. Here sat the Lord of Heaven, in the house of his friends, as the hour of his greatest trial approached, with those who loved him [Mary] knowing he was soon to face betrayal and crucifixion. What act of love, of devotion, of adoration, of worship could a mere mortal perform for him who is eternal? Could a loved one do more than David had said the Good Shepherd himself would do in conferring honor and blessing upon another, that is: 'Thou anointest my head with oil'?[23]

"To anoint the head of a guest with ordinary oil was to do him honor; to anoint his feet also was to show unusual and signal regard; but the anointing of head and feet with spikenard, and in such abundance, was an act of reverential homage rarely rendered even to kings. Mary's act was an expression of adoration; it was the fragrant outwelling of a heart overflowing with worship and affection."[24]

As we ponder and begin to understand the symbolism of

her expressive act, we come to admire and honor her sensitivity and special insight while in part fulfilling the Lord's prophecy regarding her act of love. Mary somehow knew that these were His final days. She offered Him what she could. Whether acting on her own instinct and sensitivity or on an unrecorded spiritual prompting, her actions were appropriately foretelling. Her use of oil, in this case oil of spikenard, is heavy with symbolism and stands as a solemn reminder of Christ's life and mission. Oil, specifically olive oil, is significant in both ancient and modern times. To more fully appreciate the symbolism of Mary's act and of an oil anointing, let us begin our investigation into olive oil symbolism in one historic garden and conclude in another.

The tree of life is a familiar enough concept in religious imagery and tradition. It is as ancient as the terrestrial Garden of Eden. It stood in opposition to the tree of the knowledge of good and evil, or "the tree of mortal life." In its opposing role, the tree of life was actually a tree of eternal life—the necessary opposite of mortality. As the tree of the knowledge of good and evil contained the seeds of death and mortality, so the tree of life contained the power of everlasting life. In Nephi's vision, he was shown this tree, "and it was like unto the tree which my father [Lehi] had seen; and the beauty thereof was far beyond, yea, exceeding of all beauty; and the whiteness thereof did exceed the whiteness of the driven snow" (1 Ne. 11:8). Nephi, wanting to know the meaning (symbolism) of the tree, was shown a vision of the birth of Christ with an angelic declaration, "Behold the Lamb of God, yea, even the

Son of the Eternal Father!" The angel asked, "Knowest thou
the meaning of the tree which thy father saw?" To which
Nephi replied: "Yea, it is the love of God, which sheddeth itself
abroad in the hearts of the children of men; wherefore, it is the
most desirable above all things. . . "Yea, and the most joyous
to the soul" (1 Ne. 11:21–23).

Nephi learned that Jesus is the "love of God" (John 3:16)
and that the tree of life is another symbol of Jesus Christ, our
Savior and Redeemer. The fruit of the tree of life represents
His infinite eternal Atonement and is "the greatest of all the
gifts of God" (1 Ne. 8:11, 21–22, 25; 15:36).

In the Garden of Eden, Adam and Eve accepted mortality by partaking of the mortal fruit. Afterward, they were
restricted from approaching the tree of life, "lest [Adam] put
forth his hand and partake also of the tree of life, and eat
and live forever [in his sins]" (Mos. 4:28). They were physically
prevented from approaching its presence by "cherubim and a
flaming sword, which turned every way to keep the way of the
tree of life" (Mos. 4:31). With the tree representing the Savior,
we observe in the symbolism mortality's consequential separation from God. This separation is expressed as both spiritual
and physical death. These deaths are probationary conditions
reconciled only through the Lord's Atonement. "For as in
Adam all die, even so in Christ shall all be made alive" (1 Cor.
15:22).

Salvation comes to all men born in the flesh through
the grace of Christ. This is complete redemption from physical death, a perfect resurrection. Exaltation is also received

through the grace of Christ upon conditions of repentance and obedience to the laws and commandments of His gospel. This is redemption from spiritual death. As the Lord placed "cherubim and a flaming sword" in the Garden of Eden to block the way of the tree of life, so too, in His immortal worlds, He places cherubim (prophets who have ministered to their earths) with flaming swords (the purifying and dividing light of the gospel) to discern who is prepared and qualified to return to the presence of God. "The placement of these sentinels in front of the tree of life indicates our need for the ordinances and covenants of the temple in order to regain the presence of the Father and the Son—Jesus himself being the tree of life."[25]

From the Garden of Eden, mortality and death entered the world. With the hope of another garden, a Redeemer was promised, predicted, and provided "from before the foundation of the world." It is to this other garden that all mankind must look for redemption from the consequences of mortal sin and death. It is to Gethsemane that all creation looks for the fruit of the tree of life.

The imagery and symbolism of the tree of life and its fruit are constant reminders to us of the Savior's divine act of redemption. It also foreshadows both the place of His atoning suffering and the location of the crucifixion (Acts 10:39). Lehi's vision of the tree of life and subsequent revelations on the topic do not specify a particular species of tree, but the use, imagery, and symbolism of an olive tree and of an olive vineyard in scripture and sacred history combine to offer a powerful impression of "[a] tree. . . precious above all. . . Yea, and

most joyous to the soul" (1 Ne. 11:9, 23). The olive tree, its
fruit, and especially its unique oil occupy a singular position
in history, symbolism, and religious observance.

The Mount of Olives in the meridian of time was covered
with vineyards of olive trees. The trees required great effort
over extended periods of time to cultivate their fruit. Rock
terraces were first built to retain soil and to capture precious
water; trees were planted, fertilized, pruned, grafted, culti-
vated, nurtured, and tended. Over many years, patience and
hard labor yielded olives. Even then, the fruit was not ready for
consumption. Harvested olives are bitter and hard. They must
be cured—prepared with salts and vinegar—and only then
were olives ready for the dining table.

Olives had multiple uses in ancient Israel. Not only were
they eaten, they were also the source of precious oil, which was
used in medicine, lighting, heat, and sacred anointings. "Olive
oil was the substance of light and heat in Israel. Olive lamps,
into which one poured the pure oil and then lighted it at one
end, provided, even in a darkened room, light. . . Not only all
this, but the balming influence, the soothing, salving influence of oil, was well known in their midst. . . Paul referred to
it as the oil of gladness, and it is in that sense also symbolic of
joy"[26] (Ps. 45:7; Isa. 61:3; Heb. 1:9).

Somewhere on that mount, due east of the temple, was
a place of refinement, a location of olive processing, another
garden among trees. It is called Gethsemane. "*Geth* or *gat*
means *press,* and *shemen* in Hebrew means *oil.* . . *[Gethsemane
is]* the place of the olive press."[27]

Harvested olives were prepared and brought to this place. The meat of the fruit was stripped from the pits and chopped into a mash. The broken pieces of olive flesh were placed in a cloth bag and carried to the olive press. A simple press was made of stone; usually two heavily opposing slabs of carved stone, the lower stone being raised up off the ground like a small altar. Into it was carved channels, which led to a collecting basin below where the precious oil was gathered. Onto the stone press the olive mash was laid and the heavy top stone placed upon it. To this was added pressure by means of a lever, usually a heavy tree trunk or log, which was secured or wedged in a rock close to the pressing stones. The greater length of the log extended over and across the press; to this extended lever was added heavy stones on ropes in greater and greater number along the entire length of the tree. As the weight increased, so did the pressure on the bitter olives. More weight, more pressure—crushing, oppressive, weight upon weight upon weight. Only under this immense pressure would the refining process begin, and the oil, drop by drop, begin to flow. One can imagine such an oil press at harvest time. The presses were prepared late into the evening, weight and pressure were added, more weight and more pressure were applied. The process took many hours so the bitter fruit was left to itself to be pressed out over the long dark night. While the laborers slept.

The images of Gethsemane and of the ancient olive press, the refining of precious oil—these images cry out with sacred symbolism! Oil pressed in the refining process is no longer bitter but sweet! It is light, it is pure, it has been miraculously transformed into a unique substance. It is a natural disinfectant, a universal antidote for poison, the ancient source of light and heat, of nourishment and healing. It is the Samaritan's balm, with its soothing, repairing influence on wounded limbs and lives.

Anciently, the Levitical priests of Israel in foreshadowing remembrance were commanded to "bring thee pure oil olive [that had been] *beaten for the light*" to light the lamps of the temple, "to burn always . . . [as] a statute for ever" (Exodus 27:20–21). Israel was also commanded to use pure olive oil in anointing kings and in sacred temple ordinances. "The word *messiah*, as it appears today in the King James Version of Daniel, has roots meaning the '*anointed one,*' with connotations of coronation and ordination. Now came the night when he [Christ] would become the anoint*ing* one."[28]

As the Messiah arrived at his other garden, He felt deep sorrow. He "began to be sore amazed, and to be very heavy" (Mark 14:33). On this Passover week night, the moon would have been nearly full, eventually settling low in the western sky. As the Savior left his disciples to "watch and pray," He withdrew "about a stone's cast away" into the vineyard (see chapter 4), where He would have been in the shadow of the temple. There in the Lord's vineyard, in the symbolic olive press, He suffered.

> Christ's agony in the garden is unfathomable by the finite mind, both as to intensity and cause. . . . He struggled and groaned under a burden such as no other being who has lived

on earth might even conceive as possible. It was not physical pain, nor mental anguish alone, that caused Him to suffer such torture as to produce an extrusion of blood from every pore; but a spiritual agony of soul such as only God was capable of experiencing. No other man, however great his powers of physical or mental endurance, could have suffered so; for his human organism would have succumbed. . . . In that hour of anguish Christ met and overcame all the horrors that Satan, "the prince of this world" could inflict . . . In some manner, actual and terribly real though to man incomprehensible, the Savior took upon Himself the burden of the sins of mankind from Adam to the end of the world.[29]

"The word *messias*, as it is used by John in the Gospel of John, has another root, *tsahar*, meaning to glow with light as one glistens when one is anointed." [30] That meridian night, the Lord glistened in Gethsemane with divine blood—the blood of Messiah, the Anointed One. He was anointed with "divine oil"; his own divine precious blood was pressed drop by precious drop from his immortal and sinless soul by the burden, weight, depth, and pressure of our sins. Regarding that event, Jesus explained to the Prophet Joseph Smith that His "suffering caused myself, even God, the greatest of all, to tremble because of pain, and to bleed at every pore" (D&C 19:18; see also 18:11; Mosiah 3:7).

That night the Savior drank the bitter cup—all of it. He was "beaten for the light." He was pressed and anointed with mortal sweat and immortal blood. As bitter olives are pressed sweet, our mortality, bitter sin, and death were pressed upon and swallowed up by Him. He brought forth the fruit of the tree of life, the anointing oil of the Atonement. The anointed one becoming the *anointing one*, the only one in heaven or on earth who can heal us.

After considering the tree of life and its oil symbolism, can we ever again think of olive oil in the same light? When the sick or afflicted are anointed with consecrated olive oil and blessed by his priesthood, we are being symbolically taught that it is by and through Him that the healing is possible. When we receiving our anointings in the house of the Lord, it is again by Him, through Him, and of Him that the promises are made possible and the blessings realized. When we think about the symbolic oil we need for our personal lamps and the extra oil we are required to have with us, we know it is accumulated, drop by drop, as we accept and follow Christ, applying His Atonement daily in our lives.

Do we see how the oil of the Atonement is a universal antidote for the poisons of pornography and drug addiction, a cleansing disinfectant for sins of commission and omission, and a soothing balm for wounds of hurtful relationships, both for the offender and the offended? The oil of the Atonement is our light and heat, our nourishment and balm. Without it we would be lost forever, cut off from the presence of the Lord, living in darkness without his marvelous light—and not only we, but all God's creations, infinite and eternal. All would be lost forever without Him, the "greatest of all the gifts of God" (1 Nephi 8:11), "yea, and the most joyous to the soul" (1 Nephi 11:23).

Did Mary know any of this symbolism as she reached for her alabaster container of spikenard, broke the seal, and poured the sweet-smelling oil on the head and feet of the Messiah? Perhaps it is not what she knew, but what she felt for Him that ultimately matters. "It was an act of devoted sacrifice, of exquisite self abandonment; . . . the poor Galileans who followed Jesus, so little accustomed to any luxury, so fully alive to the costly nature of the gift, might well have been amazed that it should have all been lavished on the rich luxury of one brief moment. None but the most spiritual-hearted there could feel that the delicate odor which breathed through the perfumed house might be to God a sweet-smelling savor; *that even this was infinitely too little to satisfy the love of her who gave, or the dignity of Him to whom the gift was given*" [31]

Mary's act was as the light of a single olive oil lamp, compared to the consuming fire of God's glorified, exalted presence. Her small flame might seem inconsequential and perhaps, to a lesser observer, inadequate, but both her light and His are fueled by the same source—divine oil, pressed from the tree of life, even "the love of God, which sheddeth itself abroad in the hearts of the children of men" (1 Nephi 11:22).

May His oil, the eternal light of Israel, be found in each of us at the last day so that our whole bodies may be filled with His marvelous light so that we might, through Him, be able to bear and comprehend all things (D&C 88:67).

What praises can we offer,
To thank thee, Lord most high?
In our place thou didst suffer;
In our place thou didst die.
By heaven's plan appointed,
To ransom us, our King,
O Jesus, the anointed,
To thee our love we bring!
No creature is so lowly,
No sinner so depraved,
But feels thy presence holy,
And thru thy love is saved.
Tho craven friends betray thee,
They feel thy love's embrace;
The very foes who slay thee,
Have access to thy grace.

"O Savior, Thou Who Wearest a Crown," Hymns, no.
197, verses 4, 2.

Commentary

THE SYMBOLISM OF OIL AND LIGHT

There comes a point with some tokens where the image invoked by the selected symbolism and the truth of its similitude become difficult to separate. This is the case with oil's reference to light and the symbolism of light used in the Lord's teachings. In ancient Israel, olive oil provided the only dependable and sustainable (renewable) source of light other than the sun, moon, and stars. Oil was by practice and tradition synonymous with light. Even the light in the ancient temple was fired with pure oil derived from olives "beaten for the light." Light is invoked by the Lord in His teaching, specifically in referring to Himself. For example, the Savior said, "I am the light of the world: he that followeth me shall not walk in darkness, but shall have the light of life" (John 8:12). There is symbolic intent in this passages, but it also contains a sobering literal message.

Modern scripture clarifies and provides instructive insight into the true nature and source of light. Referring to Himself, the Lord explains that He

> ascended up on high, as also he descended below all things, in that he comprehended all things, that he might be in all and through all things, the light of truth; Which truth shineth. *This is the light of Christ.* As also he is in the sun, and *the light of the sun,* and the power thereof by which it was made. As also he is in the moon, and *is the light of the moon,* and the

power thereof by which it was made; As *also the light of the stars*, and the power thereof by which they were made; And the earth also, and the power thereof, even the earth upon which you stand. *And the light which shineth, which giveth you light, is through him who enlighteneth your eyes, which is the same light that quickeneth your understandings; Which light proceedeth forth from the presence of God to fill the immensity of space*—The light which is in all things, which giveth life to all things, which is the law by which all things are governed, even the power of God who sitteth upon his throne, who is in the bosom of eternity, who is in the midst of all things. (D&C 88:6–13)

In this revelation we see that all light "proceedeth forth from the presence of God to fill the immensity of space." This is all light, all spectrums, all bandwidths, and all frequencies in all dimensions. God is literally the source of all light, both physical and spiritual, all truth and all creation. "The light which shineth . . . is through him" (D&C 88:6–13).

Light as a metaphor of Christ can be confused or misunderstood with the truth that Christ is, in fact, the literal light of the world and "the power thereof by which it was made." He is a light; in fact, He is *the* light to each of us in every sense.

As olive oil was synonymous with light in the ancient world, its symbolism can at times "blend" or dare I say "bleed" together, in the same way that the wavelengths of color in the visual spectrum combine to create brilliant white light. Olive oil, symbolic of the fruit of the tree of life, is symbolically understood as the Atonement (precious fruit) of Christ (the tree of life) which makes or enables all things to bring to pass the salvation of our Father in Heaven's children.

Light, used as a metaphor of Christ, invokes Him in its imagery and animation of life. But as a symbol, it is much more. It is both a token and the Light of Christ Himself.

As you enjoy a bright, sunny day and feel the warmth and cheeriness of radiant light, try to imagine the light's source emanating and proceeding from God's glorious presence, transmitted by heavenly bodies of the same order as our Sun, filling the immensity of space, bringing order and intelligence and governance to his numberless worlds that we can neither count nor fully comprehend. (Abr. 3:9–10; Mos. 1:4–5, 10, 27–33). We can be grateful for what we have received and rejoice in its source.

HARVESTING OLIVES

Several times I've referenced Exodus 27:20–21 when referring to olive oil and light. This passage specifically speaks to the house of Israel and the use of olive oil observances in the ancient temple. The symbolism and imagery refer to the brutality of the Atonement as represented by the harvesting of olives. When olives are gathered, the process begins at the tree. Recall the symbolic relationship between the tree of life, its fruit, and the Savior—just as Christ was beaten; the olive tree is struck with long poles to knock down the olives to begin the harvest and refining process. Because oil was the primary source of light in the ancient world, the trees were beaten for their olives and for their refined oil. The Light of the world was also beaten for his light. The harvesting of the tree of life, His precious oil, is symbolically remembered and represented by the harvesting and refining of olives.

CHAPTER 6

The Shepherd
and the Lamb

"And they must come according to the words which shall be
established by the mouth of the Lamb; and the words of the
Lamb shall be made known in the records of thy seed, as well
as in the records of the twelve apostles of the Lamb; wherefore
they both shall be established in one; for there is one God and
one Shepherd over all the earth."

—1 Nephi 13:41

THE NIGHTS WERE GETTING SHORTER AND WARMER NOW
that the spring equinox had passed. It was early spring
and the sheep were still nurturing their young lambs. Abraham
had not slept this night. At the moment he was thinking of the
new lambs. It was curious where his thoughts wandered and
what he contemplated under stress—and Abraham was sud-
denly under tremendous stress. His soul was aching with a
numbing determination that had sustained him through his
darkest night.

His thoughts again returned to the spring lambs—he
would not need one. Abraham found himself wishing that
this night would never end, but a faint thin line of bluish light

along the eastern horizon was just beginning to appear. It would soon be morning. He arose, dressed, and began to collect his provisions. He would not eat but would again pray for strength, faith, and understanding.

The Lord's command was evident and unequivocal, "Take now thy son, thine only son Isaac, whom thou lovest, and get thee into the land of Moriah; and offer him there for a burnt offering upon one of the mountains which I will tell thee" (JST Genesis 22:2).

His assignment was clear; the Lord's commandment, unmistakable. Abraham was to act and act immediately. Abraham had covenanted to live by God's every word. The Lord had declared, "Thou shalt keep the commandments which I have given thee with mine own mouth, and I will be a God unto thee and thy seed after thee" (JST Genesis 17:12). God told him to act "now." So Abraham "saddled his ass, and took two of his young men with him, and Isaac his son, and clave the wood for the burnt offering, and rose up, and went unto the place of which God had told him" (JST Genesis 22:3–4).

Mount Moriah was quite familiar to Abraham. He had visited there many times. He had paid tithes to Melchizedek, the great high priest and king of Salem (JST Genesis 14:26–28, 36). Melchizedek's translated city had been at Moriah (JST Genesis 14:34). The mount was now part of Abraham's territorial inheritance. The Lord had promised to Abraham and his seed the lands from the Nile to the Euphrates (see Genesis 17:2–13). With Melchizedek and his city's inhabitants now gone, who would reclaim the covenant land if Isaac were offered? Who would watch over, protect, and fill it as the Lord had promised?

Abraham lived almost due south of Mount Moriah near Hebron. As the little band headed north, their pace was metered by Abraham's years and the mountainous terrain. His steps were deliberate and steady, but perhaps a little slower than usual. What awaited them at Moriah was a stupefying burden. Physically, spiritually, and mentally, it was a heavy and sorrowful journey of some twenty miles up to the mount.

On the way from Hebron to Moriah, Abraham would have passed by the site of the future village of Bethlehem. It would be located on a rocky ridge just south of Jerusalem overlooking a small valley. The valley would be King David's future pasture where he tended flocks as a youth, defending his young lambs with sling and stone. Today this little valley is called Shepherd's Field. Both in David's day and at the time of Christ's birth and mortal ministry, shepherds kept watch over their flocks by night in this protective valley. It was an ideal location for shepherding because of the safety of its many limestone caves and crevasses and its proximity to the Temple Mount (Moriah). These future shepherds' herds would provide spring lambs to the temple for the annual Passover observance. In Abraham's day, this field was unattended. As Abraham approached the mountain from the south he would have first seen Moriah from this rocky ridge— the future birthplace of the Savior and the source of sacrificial lambs for temple sacrifice.

"Then on the third day Abraham lifted up his eyes, and saw the place afar off. And Abraham said unto his young men, Abide you here with the ass; and I and the lad will go yonder and worship, and come to you again. And Abraham took the wood of the burnt offering, and laid it upon his [Isaac's] back; and he took the fire in his hand, and a knife; and Isaac his son; and they went both of them together" (JST Genesis 22:5–7).

Ponder this important point, repeated twice, that, "they went both of them together." From the future Bethlehem, a patriarchal father escorted his son to a sacred place, an alter of suffering and sacrifice. "And Isaac spake unto Abraham his father, and said. . . Behold the fire and the wood: but where is the lamb for a burnt offering? And Abraham said, My son, *God will provide himself a lamb* for a burnt offering: *so they went both of them together*" (JST Genesis 22:7–8; emphasis added). The repetitive declaration speaks to their closeness, their unity, and their representative similitude as Father and Son.

The record goes on to say that "they came to the place which God had told him of" (Genesis 22: 9). It is apparent that an exact location for the offering was given to Abraham and Isaac. That the location was precise is an important commentary to the narrative in several ways. The lessons being taught to Abraham and Isaac needed to be precise, just as the future central act itself would be exact, complete, and eternal—sufficient in every way to satisfy the infinite demands of justice. An approximate location would not do. Abraham and Isaac were instructed to go to the northwest corner of the Moriah mount. There at Golgotha, in symbolic similitude, Abraham and Isaac were to be tested. It would be the concluding location of the future Messianic trials and the ultimate expression of our Savior's atoning sacrifice, his voluntary death.

Precise and foretelling also were the revelations from the premortal Messiah regarding the manner of ancient sacrifice. He instructed his prophet, "Speak unto the children of Israel, and say unto them, If any man of you bring an offering unto the Lord, ye shall bring your offering . . . of his own voluntary will at the door of the tabernacle [Temple] of the congregation before the Lord. . . . And he shall put his hand upon the head of the burnt offering; and it shall be accepted for him to make atonement for him. . . . And if his offering *be* of the flocks, *namely*, of the sheep . . . for a burnt sacrifice; he shall bring it a male without blemish. And he shall kill it on the side of the altar *northward* before the Lord: and the priests, Aaron's sons, shall sprinkle his blood round about upon the altar" (Lev. 1:2–4, 10–11; emphasis added). The "northward" orientation of the Lord's instruction to Israel points to the location of His future messianic sacrifice on Mount Moriah and also speaks to His message of exactness.

The precise location and the detailed instruction regarding the manner of sacrificial offerings resonates the importance of this similitude and the Atonement. We see today the same exactness in the revealed sacramental prayers and in the administration of temple covenants.

The whole of Abraham and Isaac's experience from Hebron to Moriah comments on the conditions of the Savior at the time of His Atonement: His sorrowful heavy journey to Golgotha, the manner and location of the Atonement, the escorting presence of His Father, and the Son's ultimate sacrifice on the altar of Moriah (this mount and this earth)—all this while teaching Abraham and Isaac, the obedient father and son, regarding the roles of our Eternal Father and His Only Begotten Son in the great plan of redemption. In every detail, Abraham and Isaac's test is elegant similitude and poignant symbolism.

What Abraham and Isaac understood of their similitude at the time they approached this sacred place is unclear. Did they know that this area would be the center of universal attention at the meridian of time, when all of God's creations would look for the signs of his birth, ministry, and mission? Prophets would testify on infinite worlds of the advent of the Savior into his condescending mortality. How many worlds witnessed his star appearing and looked forward with anticipation to his atoning redemption from physical and spiritual death? He was no doubt presented on those worlds as He was here on this earth—as the Lamb of God. The symbolic imagery of a sacrificial lamb foreshadowed the bitter reality, that the Lamb's blood was shed. Even at the first future Passover, as the firstborn of each household was spared, the cost was the life and blood of an innocent lamb.

> And they came to the place which God had told him of, and Abraham built an altar there, and laid the wood in order, and bound Isaac his son, and laid him on the altar upon the wood. And Abraham stretched forth his hand, and took the knife to slay his son. And the angel of the Lord called unto him out of heaven, and said . . . Lay not thine hand upon the lad, neither do thou any thing unto him: for now I know that thou fearest God, seeing thou hast not withheld thy son, thine only [Isaac]

son from me. . . . And Abraham called the name of that place Jehovah-jireh: as it is said to this day, In the mount of the Lord it shall be seen. (Genesis 22:9–12, 14)

In this test, Abraham's hand was stayed. A human sacrifice on the altar of Moriah would not be sufficient or required (see Alma 34:10). Again, the lesson of the similitude points to the Lamb of God that would come in the meridian of time. Abraham's declaration to Isaac, "My son, *God will provide himself a lamb*" was both prophetic and declarative. Under the same inspiration, John the Baptist would exclaim, "Behold the Lamb of God, which taketh away the sin of the world" (John 1: 29). Of our Lord's many titles, at times of greatest joy and rejoicing, we shout in anthems of praise and adoration, "Hosanna! Hosanna! Hosanna! To God and *the Lamb!*"

Abraham's trial was not only a test of his willingness *to* sacrifice but also a lesson *on* sacrifice—an invitation to all Abraham's descendants to live by every word of God's mouth, to follow the Savior's example of perfect love, compassion, long suffering, and preparations (service) unto the children of men.

To those who love Him and desire to follow His example of perfect service (by accepting His sacrifice and striving to become like Him) it is also a commentary on discipleship (see Matthew 5:48). Anciently the law of sacrifice required the offering of first fruits and the unblemished; today it requires the free-will offering of our desires, a sacrifice of self-seeking secularism, the broken heart and contrite spirit of Abraham and Isaac who lived by God's law and not their own.

Protection in this world and exaltation in the next begins

by receiving faith in Christ and by acting on that faith. We must become even as Abraham, a follower of righteousness by choice and by action (see Abr. 1:2).

In this sense, we become lambs and sheep to our personal shepherd. The Savior taught this symbolism: "I am the good shepherd: the good shepherd giveth his life for the sheep. . . and [I] know my sheep, and am known of mine. As the Father knoweth me, even so know I the Father: and I lay down my life for the sheep. . . Therefore doth my Father love me, because I lay down my life, that I might take it again. No man taketh it from me, but I lay it down of myself. I have power to lay it down, and I have power to take it again" (John 10:11, 14–15, 17–18).

Isaiah poetically prophesied that we are his sheep, saying, "He shall feed his flock like a shepherd: he shall gather the lambs with his arm, and carry them in his bosom, and shall gently lead those that are with young" (Isa. 40:11). The Savior is a Shepherd and the Lamb in the same sense that He is a Father and the Son. His central role is best understood in light of his Messianic mission. As the creator of this earth (see Ephesians 3:9), He was given power by his Father to be a God. As the premortal Messiah, He was the great I Am of the Old Testament, the lawgiver and provider of manna from heaven, the light and thunder of Sinai (see chapter 3). As the mortal Messiah, He became the Only Begotten Son of the Father in the flesh, our Advocate and Mediator with the Father, our Savior and Redeemer.

Abinadi taught, "I would that ye should understand that God himself shall come down among the children of men, and shall redeem his people. And because he dwelleth in flesh he shall be called the Son of God, and having subjected the flesh to the will of the Father, being the Father and the Son—The Father, because he was conceived [in the premortal life] by the power of God; and the Son, because of the flesh; thus becoming the Father and Son" (Mosiah 15:1–3).

He is the Lamb of God, "slain from the foundation of the world" (Rev. 13: 8; Mos. 7: 47).

Because Christ offered Himself in the premortal life as the Lamb, He received power from his Father—power to organize and preside over the Earth. As the pre-ordained Messiah, He came to his creation in the meridian of time to serve his Father's children and to redeem us from death. There is power in selfless service. Apparently the greatest power comes from the greatest sacrifice. By his Atonement, the Lord received additional power: "Worthy is the Lamb that was slain to receive power" (Rev. 5:12). As we were added upon by coming to this earth, so he, through his condescending life of selfless service, was added upon with sufficient power to claim us as his own.

He received power to become the Good Shepherd. Abinadi explained,

> And after all this, after working many mighty miracles among the children of men, he shall be led, yea, even as Isaiah said, as a sheep before the shearer is dumb, so he opened not his mouth. Yea, even so he shall be led, crucified, and slain, the flesh becoming subject even unto death, the will of the Son being swallowed up in the will of the Father. And thus God

breaketh the bands of death, having gained the victory over death; *giving the Son power to make intercession for the children of men*—Having ascended into heaven, having the bowels of mercy; being filled with compassion toward the children of men; standing betwixt them and justice; having broken the bands of death, taken upon himself their iniquity and their transgressions, having redeemed them, and satisfied the demands of justice. And now I say unto you, who shall declare his generation? Behold, I say unto you, that when his soul has been made an offering for sin he shall see his seed. And now what say ye? And who shall be his seed? (Mos. 15:6–10; emphasis added)

His seed are those who hear His voice, who come unto Him and take His name upon themselves. His seed are His sheep, the sheep of the Good Shepherd.

The king of love my Shepherd is, whose goodness faileth never; I nothing lack if I am his and he is mine forever. Where streams of living water flow, my ransomed soul he leadeth, and where the verdant pastures grow, with food celestial feedeth. Perverse and foolish oft I strayed, but yet in love he sought me, and on his shoulder gently laid, and home rejoicing brought me. In death's dark vale I fear no ill, with thee, dear Lord, beside me; Thy rod and staff my comfort still, thy cross before to guide me. Thou spread'st a table in my sight; Thy unction grace bestoweth; and O what transport of delight from thy pure chalice floweth! And so through all the length of days thy goodness faileth never: Good Shepherd, may I sing thy praise, within thy house for ever. ("The King of Love My Shepherd Is," *Hymns*, with words by Henry W. Baker)

Abraham was commanded by the Lord to sacrifice Isaac at Moriah. There his discipleship and obedience became an illuminating example of willingness to be lead. Abraham was willing to sacrifice his most treasured possession and promised blessing, his "only Isaac," to become Christ's seed. The reward for obedience is eternal abundance. In return for his faithfulness, Abraham's seed became numberless. We must in like manner be lead, even as sheep that eagerly hear and follow his voice, even if the path leads to a personal Moriah.

As Abraham and Isaac returned to the camp of his servants, they again passed Shepherds' Field; again they approached the future village of Bethlehem, the city and house of David. They would never be the same because of their experience. They, too, like a prophetic echo of the Savior's sacrifice, had been endowed with power. They had been tempered in the Lord's furnace and were strengthened and purified by their obedience. Their worthiness was confirmed by the gift and blessing of personal power. Their confidence waxed strong in the presence of the Lord. Righteousness was their constant companion, and the Spirit purified, sanctified, and justified their souls while confirming their covenants. The same covenants and blessings are active and available today to all of Abraham's posterity to bless and prepare the earth for her Shepherd King.

Abraham's obedient posterity blesses this earth with their righteousness and service. The Lord remembers his people and has promised to gather his sheep. Nephi recorded a sure promise to his Saints of this final dispensation. He said, "I beheld the power of the Lamb of God, that it descended upon the saints of the church of the Lamb, and upon the covenant people of the Lord, who were scattered upon all the face of the earth; and they were armed with righteousness and with the power of God in great glory" (1 Nephi 14:14).

Jesus Christ is both Shepherd and Lamb to all of his creations. Just as Abraham's seed are numberless, so are the worlds of our Christ. To His disciples at the temple in Bountiful He said,

> Verily, verily, I say unto you that I have other sheep, which are not of this land, neither of the land of Jerusalem, neither in any parts of that land round about whither I have been to minister. For they of whom I speak are they who have not as yet heard my voice; neither have I at any time manifested myself unto them. But I have received a commandment of the Father that I shall go unto them, and that they shall hear my voice, and shall be numbered among my sheep, that there may be one fold and one shepherd; therefore I go to show myself unto them. (3 Nephi 16:1–3)

Also speaking of the last days, Nephi expounded the prophecies of Isaiah, saying, "And the time cometh speedily that the righteous must be led. . . and the Holy One of Israel must reign in dominion, and might, and power, and great glory. And he gathereth his children from the four quarters of the earth; and *he numbereth his sheep*, and they know him; and *there shall be one fold and one shepherd; and he shall feed his sheep, and in him they shall find pasture*" (1 Nephi 22:24–25; emphasis added).

We are being gathered in these latter days, as the Lord

has promised and covenanted with Abraham, Isaac, Jacob, and Joseph. He promised, "I shall proceed to do a marvelous work among them, that I may remember my covenants which I have made unto the children of men, that I may set my hand again the second time to recover my people, which are of the house of Israel" (2 Nephi 29:1). He gathers and watches over His sheep. He seeks out the hungry and helpless and cold. He calls us to hear. He calls us to follow his voice. He calls us to serve and act and pray.

As we follow Him, we become His. Our Good Shepherd does not leave us comfortless; He leads as a shepherd leads his flock—out in front, even if we cannot see Him from where we are. As we hear His voice and respond, He comes to us. He comes in many ways. First we hear his voice, often as the voice of his servants or under-shepherds or as an answer to our deepest desire. He said, "I will not leave you comfortless: I will come to you" (John 14:18).

In our day, as prophetically foretold, the Lord has personally fulfilled His promises by reestablishing and restoring His prophets, revelation, priesthood, scripture, ordinances, temples, and covenants in the fulness of all past dispensations. Through His latter-day prophet He declared, "Wherefore, I am in your midst, and *I am the good shepherd*, and *the stone of Israel*. He that buildeth upon this rock shall never fall. And the day cometh that you shall hear my voice and see me, and know that I am. Watch, therefore, that ye may be ready. Even so. Amen" (D&C 50:44–46; emphasis added).

The Lord my pasture will prepare,
And Feed me with a shepherd's care.
His presence will my wants supply,
And guard me with a watchful eye.
My noon-day walks he will attend,
And all my silent midnight hours defend."

"The Lord My Pasture Will Prepare," Hymns,
no. 109, verse 1.

Commentary

A UNIFIED ACT OF LOVE

Jacob pointed out in his teaching and testimony of the Savior that the offering up of Abraham's son Isaac was a similitude of the sacrifice of God the Father and his Only Begotten Son (see Jacob 4:5). Recall that Abraham and Isaac approached the mount together, symbolic of Elohim and Jehovah's unified and joint commitment to accomplish the future Atonement. Jacob identified that the patriarchs' condescending similitude "points our souls to Him," to Christ, and to our Heavenly Father as their unified act of love.

The biblical record testifies that Abraham "took the wood of the burnt offering [perhaps symbolic of the future cross], and laid it upon Isaac his son." This passage echoes Isaiah's verse, "Yet it pleased the Lord to bruise him; he hath but him to grief: when thou shalt make his soul an offering for sin" (Isaiah 53:10). Isaac accepted the burden from his father and his explanation, which is also symbolic: "God will provide himself a lamb for a burnt offering" (Gen. 22:8). At some point, Abraham likely had a further and more revealing discussion with Isaac of the Lord's command and requirement. The record is silent on detail but rich is consequence. Isaac, like the Savior, accepted his father's will and condescended to both his fathers—temporal and spiritual. He was submissive and suffered the will of the fathers in all things. How fitting a similitude is Isaac of the Savior, and Abraham of the Father, unified in sacrifice and in love.

SPRING LAMBS AND THE PASSOVER

For generations, the shepherds of Israel raised spring lambs in Shepherds' Field near Bethlehem. Male lambs were used in the temple for prescribed sacrifices, but in particular they were required for the observance of the annual Passover feast in the spring of the year. The Passover observance commemorated the original Passover when a lamb without blemish or spot was slain and its blood sprinkled upon the door lintel and side posts of the homes of Israel. Passover memorialized the Lord's deliverance, his angelic protection, and the flight of Israel from Egypt. Consequently, the height of the annual Passover celebration prescribed the offering of a sacrificial lamb for each family in Israel upon the altar of the temple. Spring lambs would be taken from their mothers in Shepherds' Field and brought to the pool of Bethesda on the northeast side of the temple mount. There they were washed and corralled near the temple awaiting sundown and the beginning of Passover. The law required that the lambs be "slain . . . between sundown and total darkness [of Passover night]."[32] Numerous lambs were required. As they awaited death by sacrifice, frightened and confused, separated from their shepherd and crying for their mothers, their bleating could be heard rising over the noise of the crowded streets as all of Jerusalem awaited the beginning of Passover and the hope of a Messiah.

These were the circumstances in Jerusalem that Passover eve as the Lord made His way from Pilate's hand bowl to Golgotha. The Lamb of God, judged and condemned, was now being taken to be slain, even as the lambs from Shepherds' Field were prepared and awaiting their symbolic sacrifice. The path from Roman judgment to Golgotha passes close to Bethesda's pool. I've often wondered if the Savior heard the cries of His little lambs as He made His way to His final sacrifice.

The imagery and irony of Israel's Passover lambs combine with the symbolism of the Shepherd and the Lamb at high noon of that meridian day. Together they offer another affirming testimony, "Truly, this was the Son of God."

CHAPTER 7
Alpha and Omega

"Behold, I am Jesus Christ the Son of God. I created the heavens and the earth, and all things that in them are. I was with the Father from the beginning. . . I came unto my own, and my own received me not. And the scriptures concerning my coming are fulfilled. And as many as have received me, to them have I given to become the sons of God; and even so will I to as many as shall believe on my name, for behold, by me redemption cometh. . . I am the light and the life of the world. I am Alpha and Omega, the beginning and the end."

—3 Nephi 9:15–18

THE TITLES ALPHA AND OMEGA ARE REPEATEDLY INVOKED by the Lord when identifying Himself. They are used thirty-eight times in the standard works, but particularly in the book of Revelation and the Doctrine and Covenants in connection with the latter days. They are closely associated or linked with other symbolic words, word combinations, and metaphors. They are of course the first and last letters of the Greek alphabet, but they also correspond with the first and last letters of the Hebrew alphabet (Aleph and Tau). They also relate to the Urim and Thummim, and, as symbols, they invoke a powerful message regarding Christ and His unique eternal and infinite role.

What is the Lord teaching us in these selected titles with their layered symbolisms, related imagery, and foundational doctrine? Where does it direct our thoughts and how should it influence our actions and worship? In this chapter, we look at a few of the dimensions of our Savior as He proclaims, "Behold, I am Jesus Christ the Son of God. . . I am Alpha and Omega, the beginning and the end" (3 Nephi 9:15, 18).

In every dispensation of the earth, the Lord reveals his doctrine and his covenant. It is given in every dispensation just as it was in the beginning (see Moses 5:58). The gospel is the same truth, the same light revealed from generation to generation; it is a covenant and plan that is "everlastingly the same." This new and everlasting covenant, or "good news," is revealed through his chosen prophets, who stand at the head of each dispensation of the gospel. The revelation of truth in each dispensation often follows a societal pattern of previous prosperity and pride, decline and eventual apostasy. A pattern is revealed as dispensation prophets receive and proclaim gospel truth. As we ponder the experiences of dispensational prophets, we see common patterns.

Consider Abraham, the brother of Jared, Moses, and Joseph Smith Jr. Their calls occurred after times of deep apostasy, when their societies were living in darkness without the revealed truth and without direct revelation. These prophets sought the Lord, seeking direction or specific blessings for themselves or for their families. The brother of Jared prayed for his language to be protected (Ether 1:34–35). Abraham sought the priesthood and the blessings of his fathers (Abr.

1:4). Moses approached the Lord on Sinai and sought to know Him and His will concerning Israel. (Mos. 1:1) Joseph sought the Lord's will concerning his personal salvation and what church he should join (JS-H 1:13). All were blessed beyond their imaginations because of their faith, both in premortality and mortality (see Abr. 3:23). By faithfulness they were called to preside over and direct a dispensation of the gospel. They were chosen and called as prophets and as seers.

As a missionary in 121 BC, Ammon was asked by King Limhi if he could translate twenty-four gold plates found by an expedition searching for the city of Zarahemla. Ammon could not translate the record of this fallen people. He was not a seer, but he explained that another, King Mosiah, could translate the strange engravings. Ammon explained,

> I can assuredly tell thee, O king [Limhi], of a man that can translate the records; for he has wherewith [an Urim and Thummim] that he can look, and translate all records that are of ancient date; and it is a gift from God. And the things are called interpreters, and no man can look in them except he be commanded, lest he should look for that he ought not and he should perish. And whosoever is commanded to look in them, the same is called seer. . . . And Ammon said that a seer is a revelator and a prophet also; and a gift which is greater can no man have. . . . Thus God has provided a means that man, through faith, might work mighty miracles; therefore he becometh a great benefit to his fellow beings. (Mosiah 8:13, 16, 18)

The Bible Dictionary states that Urim and Thummim are Hebrew terms that mean "Lights and Perfections." They are

an instrument prepared of God to assist man in obtaining revelation from the Lord and in translating languages. (Ex. 28:30; Lev. 8:8; Num. 27:21; Deut. 33:8; 1 Sam. 28:6; Ezra 2:63; Neh. 7:65; JS-H 1:35) Using an Urim and Thummim is the special prerogative of a seer, and it would seem reasonable that such instruments were used from the time of Adam. However, the earliest mention is in connection with the brother of Jared (Ether 3:21–28). Abraham used an Urim and Thummim (Abr. 3:1–4), as did Aaron and the priests of Israel, and also the prophets among the Nephites (Omni 1:20–21; Mosiah 8:13–19; 21:26–28; 28:11–20; Ether 4:1–7). There is more than one Urim and Thummim, but we are informed that Joseph Smith had the one used by the brother of Jared (Ether 3:22–28; D&C 10:1; 17:1). A partial description is given in JS-H 1:35. Joseph Smith used it in translating the Book of Mormon and in obtaining other revelations.[33]

Joseph Smith was especially excited when he received his Urim and Thummim. He said,

'Do not be uneasy mother, all is right—see here, I have got a key,' he said, and handed her an object covered with a silk handkerchief. . . . After breakfast Joseph called Joseph Knight into another room and, with the happy enthusiasm of a young man, told him that everything was 'ten times Better then I expected.' He described the plates but was more excited about the Urim and Thummim: 'I can see any thing; they are Marvelus.'[34]

Joseph included a description of that Urim and Thummim in his history: "there were two stones in silver bows—and these stones, fastened to a breastplate, constituted what is called the Urim and Thummim—[they were] deposited with the plates; and the possession and use of these stones were what constituted 'seers' in ancient or former times; and. . . God had prepared them for the purpose of translating the book" (JS-H 1:35) We know that the Urim and Thummim could be fastened to a breastplate when used for judgment, as described in the Old Testament (see Ex. 28:30).

A seer receives revelation through the Urim and Thummim to teach and judge his people. A seer represents the Savior as His authorized prophet and as a presiding high priest. Alpha and Omega (Greek) and the two letters Aleph and Tau (Hebrew) were associated with the high priest of the ancient temple. In the first chapter of the book of Revelation, the Savior is also presented as the high priest of the heavenly temple. Alpha (Aleph/Urim) and Omega (Tau/Thummim) are associated or connected to Him. On the breastplate of judgment, Urim commenced with the letter Aleph and the Thummim with the letter Tau. As the seer inquired of and received answers from Jehovah, it is believed the Urim would alight to signify a positive response and the Thummim would darken to signify a negative one.[35]

So Alpha and Omega, along with Aleph and Tau, suggest the idea of Christ being "the first and the last." They are directly linked to the Urim and Thummim or to "Lights and Perfections" and with the statements of the Lord referring to Himself as the "life and light of the world." When the resurrected Lord appeared in the Americas, He presented Himself thus:

> Behold, I am Jesus Christ the Son of God. I created the heavens and the earth, and all things that in them are. I was with the Father from the beginning. I am in the Father, and the Father in me; and in me hath the Father glorified his name. I came unto my own, and my own received me not. And the scriptures concerning my coming are fulfilled. And as many as have received me, to them have I given to become the sons of God; and even so will I to as many as shall believe on my name, for behold, by me redemption cometh, and in me is the law of Moses fulfilled. *I am the light and the life of the world. I am Alpha and Omega, the beginning and the end."* (3 Ne. 9:15–18; emphasis added)

The Lord has also provided further instructional insight into his eternal nature. Moses was a dispensational prophet and no doubt a powerful seer. It was his privilege to walk and talk with the Savior face to face, "and the glory of God was upon Moses; therefore Moses could endure his presence. And God spake unto Moses, saying: Behold, I am the Lord God Almighty, and Endless is my name; for *I am without beginning of days or end of years*; and is not this endless?" Then He showed Moses the "workmanship of mine hands; but not all, for *my works are without end*, and also my words, for they never cease" (Mos. 1:2–4; emphasis added). To Enoch, Jehovah declared, "Behold, I am God; Man of Holiness is my name; Man of Counsel is my name; and *Endless and Eternal is my name, also*" (Mos. 7:35; emphasis added).

In these revelations, we understand that Jehovah is eternal, without beginning or end. We are also eternal in our elementary nature. The Lord revealed through the prophet Joseph that "man was also in the beginning with God. Intelligence, or the light of truth, was not created or made, neither indeed can be. All truth is independent in that sphere in which God has placed it, to act for itself, as all intelligence also; otherwise there is no existence" (D&C 93:29–30). Eternal existence has no beginning or end. Our existence is eternal, just as God is eternal. This is deep but basic doctrine, but what could be more fundamental to our faith and understanding during this earthly estate than knowing the true eternal nature of God and our relationship with Him?

How are we then to understand this seeming contradiction that Jehovah is eternal, yet presents Himself to us as Alpha and Omega, the beginning and the end? If we consider his declarations as symbolic teaching and testimony, we can begin to understand both his eternal nature and his intended message. As we align and examine the associated titles and terms, together they reveal a pattern and perhaps an explanation of what our Savior means as a beginning and an end.

Alpha aligns with Aleph, Lights, and light. John the Beloved taught this in his Gospel. Referring to a beginning he testified, "In the beginning was the Word [Christ], and the Word was with God [The Father], and the Word was God. *The same was in the beginning* with God. All things were made by him; and without him was not any thing made that was made" (John 1:1–4; emphasis added). John was teaching and testifying about Christ, his Master, and was speaking to us, all those who would look to Christ for redemption according to the great plan of happiness.

It was this plan that was presented to us in our premortal life state—even before the world of spirits, where we existed as eternal intelligences. There we were without "light" and without organization; we were "unordered" and unable to order or organize ourselves. John continued: "In him was life; and the life was the light of men. And the light shineth in darkness; and the darkness comprehended it not." We could not fully comprehend the Light of the Gods (the Father and the Son), who offered us the opportunity to voluntarily cooperate with Him to order or organize ourselves. Our progression in His great plan of happiness began with God the Father and His Son: the Light; the light of truth, the Word of the Lord proclaiming the opportunity to become His sons and His daughters. We are organized, ordered, animated, energized, or enabled by Him; we aligned with God and "continued" by His light; by the "Word" of truth. Using our agency to choose a path through obedience and the grace of Christ leads to an exalted end.

The letter Omega aligns with Tau, Perfections, and with (eternal) life. Our progress will end with Omega, with completeness, with "Perfections" if we continue to follow the light of truth who first ordered and enabled our progression. We see this foundational doctrine expressed in the Lord's stated mission: "This is my work and my glory—to bring to pass the immortality and eternal life of man" (Mos. 1:39).

He has identified His "glory" as intelligence: "Behold, here is the agency of man, and here is the condemnation of man; *because that which was from the beginning is plainly manifest unto them*, and they receive not the light. . . *The glory of God is intelligence*, or, in other words, light and truth" (D&C 93:31, 36; emphasis added).

This begs the question: to what intelligence is He referring? His divine intelligence of perfect submissiveness and obedience, or the intelligences (us) that have co-existed eternally and whom He labors to exalt? Perhaps His mission requires the necessary combination of the two to complete and accomplish His work of progression, redemption, and exaltation.

Is this the truth expressed in sealing power? The necessity of binding each other together in eternity to receive a fulness of joy. The binding of all "intelligences" to the Father's celestial family is the "purpose and design of our existence"; the ultimate expression of joy is becoming one with the Father through the Son.

We are central to the Father's work and glory. And because we are imperfect, the Savior and His infinite Atonement are also central to His plan of happiness, a solution necessitated by our eternal moral agency. God's mission states that He strives to bring to pass our "immortality and eternal life." His mission statement articulates the principle of God and man coming together. It is an expression of how God accomplishes His work. God "orders" or organizes eternal intelligences who, exercising their agency, choose to harmonize, cooperate, resonate, and act in the pattern and according to the Lord's eternal and unchanging commands.

What began for us as *light*, through obedience to the Lord's commandments can lead to and end for us in *perfection*. Is it any wonder that Christ is and has been from the beginning at the center of our progressive existence as the Alpha and Omega?

The universe that we observe is ordered (created or organized) by God according to His intelligence (truth and light) and includes infinite individual intelligences that co-exist with God. Read again what Joseph received by revelation, "Man was also in the beginning with God. Intelligence, or the light of truth, was not created or made, neither indeed can be. All truth is independent in that sphere in which God has placed it, to act for itself, as all intelligence also; otherwise there is no existence" (D&C 93:29–30).

As we follow our "Lights" from the beginning of our journey to exaltation, we show faith by accepting the truth, light, knowledge, and commandments we are given. Our acceptance is expressed in the form of covenants. As we align ourselves with God's light and truth, we become one with and cooperate with other intelligences that are independent in that sphere in which God has placed them, to act for themselves. Through agency we cooperate and are organized with other intelligences in the universe. In this way, the universe is ordered by God. He commands, and the intelligences (elements) obey. The obedient are added upon or somehow combined through progressive cooperation according to the law (truth) they have received.

And unto every kingdom is given a law; and unto every law there are certain bounds also and conditions. All beings [intelligences] who abide not in those conditions are not justified. *For intelligence cleaveth unto intelligence; wisdom receiveth wisdom; truth embraceth truth; virtue loveth virtue; light cleaveth unto light*; mercy hath compassion on mercy and claimeth her own; justice continueth its course and claimeth its own; judgment goeth before the face of him who sitteth upon the throne and governeth and executeth all things. He comprehendeth all things, and all things are before him, and all things are round about him; and he is above all things, and in all things, and is through all things, and is round about all things; and all things are by him, and of him, even God, forever and ever. (D&C 88:38–41; emphasis added)

Here we see the elements in cooperation, under the direction of and in harmony with God. Accordingly, the vast majority of the universe obeys the laws of the Lord and keeps His commandments by covenant.

The law of God is beautiful and harmonizing. Listen for the poetry and beauty of this description from section 88 of the Doctrine and Covenants, which Joseph Smith called the "Olive Leaf. . . plucked from the Tree of Paradise, the Lord's message of Peace to us":

And again, verily I say unto you, he hath given a law unto all things, by which they move in their times and their seasons; And their courses are fixed, even the courses of the heavens and the earth, which comprehend the earth and all the planets. And they give light to each other in their times and in their seasons, in their minutes, in their hours, in their days, in their weeks, in their months, in their years—all these are one year with God, but not with man. The earth rolls upon her wings, and the sun giveth his light by day, and the moon giveth her light by night, and the stars also give their light, as they roll upon their wings in their glory, in the midst of the power of God. Unto what shall I liken these kingdoms, that ye may understand? Behold, all these are kingdoms, and any man who hath seen any or the least of these hath seen God moving in his majesty and power. (D&C 88:42–47)

God the Eternal Father and His Son, Jehovah, are the authors of this harmony. In this life we must look to the Savior as the God of this earth, the creator, and director (see Eph. 3:9). He ordered its creation and stood among the spirits to explain the order of intelligences. He is central to our order, our progression, and our ultimate destiny.

To Abraham He explained,

If there be two spirits, and one shall be more intelligent than the other, yet these two spirits, notwithstanding one is more intelligent than the other, have no beginning; they existed before, they shall have no end, they shall exist after, for they are gnolaum, or eternal. And the Lord said unto me: These two facts do exist, that there are two spirits, one being more intelligent than the other; there shall be another more intelligent than they; *I am the Lord thy God, I am more intelligent than they all.* . . I dwell in the midst of them all; I now, therefore, have come down unto thee to declare unto thee the works which my hands have made, wherein my wisdom excelleth them all, for I rule in the heavens above, and in the earth beneath, in all wisdom and prudence, over all the intelligences thine eyes have seen from the beginning; I came down in the beginning in the midst of all the intelligences thou hast seen. (Abr. 3:18–19, 21; emphasis added)

The use of the phrasing "*I am*" in the declaration "I am more intelligent than they all" is worthy of comment. The Messiah declared Himself the great I AM in the Old Testament. It is a singular title and not insignificant. As the mortal Messiah He said, "*I am* the way, the truth, and the life: no man cometh unto the Father, but by me" (John 14:6; emphasis added). On other occasions He said, "*I am* the Lord thy God" and "*I am* Alpha and Omega."

The Savior, Jesus Christ is unique. He is more intelligent than us all. He was preeminent among the premortal spirits; called, set apart, and appointed the Atoning One; "slain before the foundation of the world." He was unique in mortality, having life in Himself as the Only Begotten Son of our Eternal Father in the flesh. He retained the capacity to die, with the power to rise again. In His own words He proclaims His role and mission "from the beginning" as Alpha and Omega, our beginning and our end, our Lights and Perfections, our light and life by obedience, the author and finisher of our salvation, the key to our exaltation and perfection. He is the Holy One.

"That which is of God is light; and he that receiveth light, and continueth in God, receiveth more light; and that light groweth brighter and brighter until the perfect day" (D&C 50:24).

Just as the seaming contradiction between God's eternal nature and His role as Alpha and Omega can be reconciled and harmonized in the Savior, even so are all things perfected in Him. All the prophets in every dispensation have testified of Him and His central role. They have all invited us to look to God, to follow the light, to come unto Christ, to be perfected in and by and through Him.

John the Beloved testified of Christ's beginning. John the Revelator also beheld in vision and described the end of this world:

> I saw a new heaven and a new earth: for the first heaven and the first earth were passed away; and there was no more sea. And I John saw the holy city, new Jerusalem, coming down from God out of heaven, prepared as a bride adorned for her husband. And I heard a great voice out of heaven saying, Behold, the tabernacle of God is with men, and he will dwell with them, and they shall be his people, and God himself shall be with them, and be their God. And God shall wipe away all tears from their eyes; and there shall be no more death, neither sorrow, nor crying, neither shall there be any more pain: for the former things are passed away. And he that sat upon the throne said, Behold, I make all things new. And he said unto me, Write . . . *I am Alpha and Omega, the beginning and the end.* I will give unto him that is athirst of the fountain of the water of life freely. He that overcometh shall inherit all things; and I will be his God, and he shall be my son. (Rev. 21:1–7)

Yes, say, what is truth? 'Tis the brightest prize
    prize
To which mortals or Gods can aspire.
Go search in the depths where it glittering
    lies,
Or ascend in pursuit to the loftiest skies:
'Tis an aim for the noblest desire.
Then say, what is truth? 'Tis the last and
    the first,
For the limits of time it steps o'er.
Tho the heavens depart and the earth's
    fountains burst,
Truth, the sum of existence, will weather
    the worst,
Eternal, unchanged, evermore.

"Oh, Say What Is Truth," Hymns, no. 272, verses
    2, 4.

Afterword

"And in the days of these kings shall the God of heaven [Jesus] set up a kingdom, which shall never be destroyed: and the kingdom shall not be left to other people, but it shall break in pieces and consume all these kingdoms, and it shall stand for ever."

—Daniel 2:44

H IS COMMON GIVEN NAME IN MORTALITY WAS TO BE JESUS, which is the modern translation of the Hebrew *Yeshua*, meaning "Jehovah is salvation." This name is also found in the forms of Jeshua, Jehoshua, and Joshua. The Joshua of the Egyptian exodus was a craftsman, a laborer, and a stonecutter—perhaps symbolic of the Lord's mortal vocation and invocative of the symbolic stone cut out of the mountain without hands in these latter days.

Daniel's revelatory vision is prophetically symbolic:

And in the days of these kings shall the God of heaven [Jesus] set up a kingdom, which shall never be destroyed: and the kingdom shall not be left to other people, but it shall break in pieces and consume all these kingdoms, and it shall stand for ever. Forasmuch as thou sawest that the stone was cut out of the mountain without hands, and that it brake in pieces the iron, the brass, the clay, the silver, and the gold; the great God [Jehovah] hath made known to the king what shall come to pass hereafter: and the dream is certain, and the interpretation thereof sure. (Dan. 2:44–45)

Perhaps the symbolism of a stonecutter in the given name of our Lord foreshadowed in part the latter-day advent of his kingdom on earth, as it was "cut out of the mountain" by His own hand, thus initiating the beginning of this last and final dispensation.

We live in the dispensation of the fulness of times, the age when there would be gathered together in one, all the elements of the previous dispensations. We live in an age of unprecedented light. The fulness of the gospel is being restored in all its majesty and beauty. Symbolic teaching and imagery are a powerful part of the message of the restoration and of a testimony of Christ.

We have considered only a few of our Savior's names and symbols in the preceding chapters. As we think about His life and His mission, the images invoked by His symbols invite reverence, worship, gratitude, and a sense of wonder. Perhaps we need these symbols because words alone are not enough to express the deep feelings we receive from the Spirit. When prophets use His symbols in their teaching and revelations, the results are beautiful. This poetry of symbolism is contained throughout the scriptures and because of modern revelation is especially available today.

Consider the following two passages, one from the Book of Mormon and one from the Bible. When pondered in light of their symbolic imagery, they resonate together to strengthen our testimony and our appreciation for symbolic teaching. They stand as poetic witnesses of Him—special symbols the Lord Jesus Christ selected to represent His life and mission—while inviting us to ponder anew His sacrifice and our relationship with Him.

The prophet Alma testified of Christ by saying,

> Behold, he sendeth an invitation unto all men, for the arms of mercy are extended towards them, and he saith: Repent and I will receive you. Yea, he saith: Come unto me and ye shall partake of the *fruit* of the *tree of life*; yea, ye shall eat and drink of the *bread* and the *waters* of life freely . . . Behold, I say unto you, that the *good shepherd* doth call you; yea, and in his own name he doth call you, which is the name of Christ; and if ye will not hearken unto the voice of the *good shepherd*, to the name by which ye are called, behold, ye are not the *sheep* of the *good shepherd*. (Alma 5:33–34, 38; emphasis added)

Jeremiah prophesied concerning the last days,

> For there shall be a day, that the watchmen upon the mount Ephraim shall cry, Arise ye, and let us go up to Zion unto the Lord our God. . . . Hear the word of the Lord, O ye nations, and declare it in the isles afar off, and say, He that scattered Israel will gather him, and keep him, as a *shepherd* doth his flock. . . . Therefore they shall come and sing in the height of Zion, and shall flow together to the goodness of the Lord, for *wheat [bread]*, and for *wine*, and for *oil*, and for the *[lamb]* young of the flock and of the herd: and their soul shall be as a *watered* garden; and they shall not sorrow any more at all. (Jer. 31:6, 10, 12; emphasis added)

Our lives can also become symbols of the Savior as we desire, seek, receive, act, and radiate the Light and Love of Christ daily in our lives. How great, how glorious, how complete we will be if we follow His path of perfections!

"Cry out and shout, thou inhabitant of Zion; for great is the Holy One of Israel in the midst of thee." (2 Ne. 22: 6).

All glory, laud and honor be to God the Eternal Father for the infinite gift of His Son! Jesus is the God of Abraham, Isaac, Jacob and Joseph; the *Living Waters* and the *Bread of Life*; the *Stone of Israel*, a tried stone, a precious cornerstone, a sure foundation; the *Fruit of the Tree of Life*; the *Shepherd of Israel* and *the Lamb* slain from before the foundation of the world; *Alpha and Omega*, the first and last, the beginning and the end; our Savior and Messiah, the Holy One!

How great the wisdom and the love
That filled the courts on high,
And sent the Savior from above
To suffer, bleed, and die.
He marked the path and led the way,
And every point defines
To light and life and endless day
Where God's full presence shines.
How great, how glorious, how complete,
Redemption's grand design,
Where justice, love and mercy meet
In harmony divine!

"How Great the Wisdom and the Love," Hymns,
no. 195, verses 1, 4, 6

Endnotes

PREFACE

[1] Frederic W. Farrar, *The Life of Christ* (London: Cassell, Limited, 1883), 393.

CHAPTER 1

[2] "The Family: A Proclamation to the World" was read by President Gordon B. Hinckley as part of his message at the General Relief Society meeting held September 23, 1995, in Salt Lake City, Utah.

[3] Bruce R. McConkie, *Doctrinal New Testament Commentary Volume 1, The Gospel* (Salt lake City: Bookcraft, 1965), 718–19.

CHAPTER 2

[4] Bible Dictionary, *LDS Scriptures* (Salt Lake City: Corporation of the President of The Church of Jesus Christ of Latter-day Saints, 1979), "Samaria, Samaritans," 768.

[5] Bruce R. McConkie, *Doctrinal New Testament Commentary Volume 1, The Gospels* (Salt lake City: Bookcraft, 1965), 151.

[6] Ibid.

[7] Ibid., 157

[8] Ibid., 155

9 Bruce R. McConkie, *Mormon Doctrine* (Salt Lake City: Bookcraft, 1966), 331.

10 Bible Dictionary, *LDS Scriptures* (Salt Lake City: Corporation of the President of The Church of Jesus Christ of Latter-day Saints, 1979), "Samaria, Samaritans," 768.

CHAPTER 3

11 Bible Dictionary, *LDS Scriptures* (Salt Lake City: Corporation of the President of The Church of Jesus Christ of Latter-day Saints, 1979), "Manna," 728–29.

12 James E. Talmage, *Jesus the Christ* (Salt Lake City: Deseret Book, 1983), 322.

13 Ibid., 310.

14 Ibid., 311.

15 Ibid., 318.

16 James E. Talmage, *The Articles of Faith* (Salt Lake City: Deseret Book, 1990), 97.

17 James E. Talmage, *Jesus the Christ* (Salt Lake City: Deseret Book, 1983), 311.

18 Bruce R. McConkie, *Doctrinal New Testament Commentary Volume 1, The Gospel* (Salt lake City: Bookcraft, 1965), 361.

CHAPTER 4

19 Bible Dictionary, *LDS Scriptures* (Salt Lake City: Corporation of the President of The Church of Jesus Christ of Latter-day Saints, 1979), "Feasts." 672–74.

20 Ibid.

21 M. Garfield Cook, *Cornerstones of the Restoration* (Salt Lake

City: Hiller Book, 1998), 117.

[22] Ibid., 122.

CHAPTER 5

[23] Bruce R. McConkie, *Doctrinal New Testament Commentary Volume 1 The Gospel* (Salt lake City: Bookcraft, 1965), 700.

[24] James E. Talmage, *Jesus the Christ* (Salt Lake City: Deseret Book, 1983), 476.

[25] Alonzo L. Gaskill, *The Lost Language of Symbolism* (Salt Lake City: Deseret Book, 2003), 300.

[26] Truman G. Madsen, *The Olive Press* (Provo: BYU Speeches, 1982), 2–3.

[27] Ibid., 3

[28] Ibid., 3–4.

[29] James E. Talmage, *Jesus the Christ* (Salt Lake City: Deseret Book, 1983), 568–69.

[30] Truman G. Madsen, *The Olive Press* (Provo: BYU Speeches, 1982), 4.

[31] Frederic W. Farrar, *The Life of Christ* (London: Cassell 1883), 329; emphasis added.

CHAPTER 6

[32] Bible Dictionary, *LDS Scriptures* (Salt Lake City: Corporation of the President of The Church of Jesus Christ of Latter-day Saints, 1979), "Feasts," 672–74.

CHAPTER 7

[33] Bible Dictionary, *LDS Scriptures* (Salt Lake City: Corporation

of the President of The Church of Jesus Christ of Latter-day Saints, 1979), "Urim and Thummim," 786–87.

[34] Richard Lyman Bushman, *Joseph Smith Rough Stone Rolling* (New York City: Knopf, 2005), 59–60.

[35] Jewish Encyclopedia, online, "Urim and Thummim." http://www.jewishencyclopedia.com/articles/14609-urim-and-thummim. Access date: 5/11/12.

Acknowledgments

ONE SNOWY DAY IN JANUARY, I FOUND A RARE SUNDAY without church meetings or assignments. Even a small amount of snow in North Carolina can stop civilization as we know it. Recently I had been introduced to and was impressed with the artistry of Jeff Hein and began to write notes about one of his newest paintings. I thank Jeff for his support and his generous permission to use of his art images in this work. I also thank the other artists, Nathan Pinnock and Michael Malm for their permission to include their works. As I began the first chapter entitled "Stone," I never intend to write a book. Later that year I showed the manuscript to Heber and Ardeth Kapp. Their encouragement kept me writing and motivated me to ponder the sources of common symbols and imagery. As the chapters multiplied, I found that the manuscript roughly followed the events in the Gospel of John. This beloved Apostle faithfully recorded critical testimony of events that would have been lost was if not for his writings. Over 90 percent of his testimony is unique to his Gospel. I am grateful to John for his faithful record and his continuing service.

While trying to express my own thoughts and impressions, I drew heavily on scriptural sources, modern gospel authorities and scholars for their insights. They include Elders Bruce R. McConkie and James E. Talmage, Brothers Truman G. Madsen, M. Garfield Cook and the Reverend Frederic W. Farrar. In several circumstances I've quoted their words because they spoke so eloquently. Other times, I combined scriptural text with my own commentary to present the circumstances of how and where the Lord introduced His symbols and their imagery. Often thoughts and impressions would occur to me as I researched and pondered sources. Consequently, this work is collaboration with many witnesses who faithfully recorded, commented or participated in these sacred events. To them, I express my deep gratitude and appreciation. Any faults, mis-statements or omissions in this work are mine alone and do not represent the position of any church or ecclesiastical authority.

I acknowledge and appreciate those who have assisted to advise, proofread, edit, suggest, comment, format, pub-lish, promote, and distribute this book. They include my best friend and companion Patti Amacher, Grant Amacher, Heber and Ardeth Kapp, Wendy (Watson) Nelson, Cory Maxwell, Dan Hogan, Angie Workman, Catherine Christensen, Emily Chambers, Rebecca Greenwood, Shawnda Craig, and Josh Johnson.

A special thanks to Ardeth Kapp for her enthusiasm, energy, support and insight. Her offer to write the Foreword to this book was both unexpected and greatly appreciated.

"Finally, as a new "author" I wanted to share an unex-pected personal insight regarding an affinity for a man I rarely thought about before—the prophet Mormon. As I studied and worked on the manuscript, my ponderings turned to thoughts of gratitude and reverence for his academic experience. He also lived during a time of increasing wickedness. He read extensively and organized inspired scriptures and writings, adding at times his own thoughts and commentary. His book, at least the parts that we have received, was an abridgement, not the original works. He quickly acknowledged his weakness with writing words and expressed his frustration over adequately covering the amount of material. In a similar way I feel more like an editor or organizer of this book. Not the creator. There is always more to say, better ways to say it.

But the symbols are pure, simple, and undeniable. They are "His." Although the symbols taught were all presented by the Savior, He taught only what He had received from His Father. If you have learned anything from this work, acknowledge Him, in the name of the Son, returning thanks for all that He has done as the Author of the great plan of redemption. Any credit for *The Savior's Symbols* belongs (remains) with Father, the Author of All.

About the Author

MARK A. AMACHER was raised in a military family, moving frequently from one duty station to another. His family eventually settled in Bountiful, Utah, during the Vietnam War. After serving as a Mormon missionary, Mark married Patti Allen in Salt Lake City while completing his university education. During a successful business career with General Electric, American International Group, and QBE of Australia, Mark and Patti moved often and traveled frequently while starting or managing businesses from Asia to the Middle East. He retired in 2011 but remains active as an industry advisor. Mark served in the Greensboro, North Carolina Stake presidency from 1996–2010 where he and Patti watched each of their three sons serve two-year missions in Oregon, California, and Louisiana. The Amachers currently serve as Church service missionaries and temple workers and reside in North Carolina. They just welcomed their first grandchild, Audrey, to the family!

About the Artists

J EFFREY HEIN WAS BORN Nov. 13, 1974 in New Windsor, New York. Since his early youth, he was interested in art and spent much of his childhood drawing. In 1992, Jeff took his first drawing classes at Ricks College, Idaho. After only one year of schooling, Jeff took three years off from his art studies to save for and then serve

a two-year mission for his church. After about twenty-one months of service, he was diagnosed with cancer and set out on several years of treatment and recovery. Jeff believes his life experiences have helped him to reach his goals as an artist and have inspired much of his work. After marrying his wife Jennifer, Hein resumed study at the University of Utah from 1998–2002. He has been painting professionally since 2002.

Jeff shows his work worldwide through Wendt Galley and has been invited to participate in a variety of international shows including the US Artist Show in Philadelphia, the Bridge Art Fair in London, and the New York Armory Show. He has been written up in numerous newspapers and national magazines, such as *Arts and Antiques*, *American Art*

Collector, Southwest Art, and in a 2005, a complimentary review by the renowned art critic John Spike. His work is in numerous private and public collections such as that of the Springville Museum of Art, Senator Gordon Smith of Oregon and Governor Mitt Romney, and The Church of Jesus Christ of Latter-day Saints.

Jeff Currently lives and works in Salt Lake City with his wife and three children. He is devoted to continual growth as an artist and when not spending time with family, he is working in his downtown studio where he divides his work time between painting, drawing, and sculpting. Jeff has also taught painting and drawing privately since 2002 and has become in high demand. In January 2007, he officially opened the Hein Academy of Art, where he currently apprentices about thirty aspiring artists.

MICHAEL MALM LIVES in the beautiful Cache Valley of northern Utah with his wife, Juanita, and their four children. The surrounding rural communities and setting provide backdrops for his figure paintings and inspiration for his landscapes. Though he paints a variety of subject matter, his first love is painting the figure. "The human figure,

in my mind, is the most beautiful of all God's creations. So much can be communicated through the tilt of the head, or the gesture of a hand. I strive to capture subtle things such as these in hopes of creating something emotional and moving."

Michael's serious study began under Del Parson at Dixie College where his completed his associate's degree. He then went on to Southern Utah University where he had the opportunity to study with Perry Stewart. Though he feels he will always be a student of painting, he completed his formal education at Utah State University where he received a Master of Fine Arts Degree studying under Glen Edwards. "I am grateful to have studied under some great artists. I was so impressed (and still am) with their work as professionals, and their ability and willingness to pass along their knowledge to me. They were very encouraging and optimistic about making a career in art because they themselves were doing it, and doing it well. I still find encouragement and inspiration in seeing their work." Michael also feels fortunate to have studied under other great painters who have had an impact on his own work. These include Richard Schmid, Burt Silverman, Dan Gerhartz, Quang Ho, Michael Workman, CW Mundy, and Jim Norton. "I have truly been blessed to have had the opportunity to have studied with some of the best living artists today. They have all been so generous with their knowledge and I will forever be grateful for their willingness to share."

NATHAN ANDREW PINNOCK IS AN ARTIST WITH A gift for capturing character in his paintings. He loves to paint people and to portray the qualities that make each person unique—to make them "come alive" through his paintings. He strives to capture situations and perspectives that the viewer may not have imagined; to celebrate the beauty in both the simple and grand moments in life.

Nathan has a rich, broad experience in art. He is often commissioned by both private and corporate collectors. He earned a bachelor of fine arts from Brigham Young University. He has also studied art at the University of Utah, Atelier LeSueur, and Utah State University.

As early as he can remember, Nathan has loved to draw, to experiment—to create. He has always had a passion for art, and couldn't imagine himself doing anything else with his life. Nate is an avid reader, and he loves to learn about universal laws, about life, and to apply these principles in his art. He enjoys studying the works of Rembrandt, Bougereau, and turn-of-the-century illustrators.

Nate is a native of Utah and currently lives in Holladay, Utah, with his wife and six children.